Inside Star Vision

Inside
Star
Star *Planetary Awakening*
and Self-Transformation
Vision

Ellias & Theanna Lonsdale

North Atlantic Books
Berkeley, California

To Ellevera Shane
Because she is really here,
on the deep inside,
where stars shine.

Inside Star Vision

Copyright © 2000 by Ellias Lonsdale. All rights reserved. No portion of this book, except for brief review, may be reproduced, stored in a retrieval system, or transmitted in any form or by any means—electronic, mechanical, photocopying, recording, or otherwise—without written permission of the publisher. For information contact North Atlantic Books.

Published by
North Atlantic Books
P.O. Box 12327
Berkeley, California 94712

Cover drawing by Harry Robins
Cover digital art by Ayelet Maida, A/M Studios
Chart illustration by Oceanna
Cover and book design by Ayelet Maida, A/M Studios
Printed in the United States of America

Inside Star Vision is sponsored by the Society for the Study of Native Arts and Sciences, a nonprofit educational corporation whose goals are to develop an educational and crosscultural perspective linking various scientific, social, and artistic fields; to nurture a holistic view of arts, sciences, humanities, and healing; and to publish and distribute literature on the relationship of mind, body, and nature.

Library of Congress Cataloging-in-Publication Data
Lonsdale, Ellias, 1947–
    Inside star vision : planetary awakening and self-transformation / Ellias Lonsdale.
       p. cm.
    ISBN 1-55643-324-7
    1. Astrology 2. Self-realization—Miscellanea. 3. Lonsdale, Theanna, d. 1993 (Spirit) I. Title.
BF1729.S38 .L66 2000
133.5—dc21   00-039436
1 2 3 4 5 6 7 8 9 / 04 03 02 01 00

Contents

Biographical Embodiment
through the Example of
Sara Lonsdale, Theanna Vivyen

Acknowledgments and Special Notes

This book opens a door to a new way to work with the stars. When we do charts, we draw up a regular star chart—tropical, geocentric, with Koch houses—and we examine the chart secondarily through traditional rulerships and patterns, primarily through the lens of the twelve Life Streams and their quickening pulse.

The simplest way to work with this method is to locate key planets in the chart and to sense which Life Streams are outstanding. If, for example, the planet Venus is leading the pattern of all the planets put together, and there is a gathering of planets in Taurus, and the first House is fully occupied, the first Life Stream will be very active and pivotal in this life's destiny.

During the last twenty-four years, we have refined this method considerably. We hope to make more of this public in a later book. *Inside Star Vision* introduces a way of seeing the stars and their workings in our destiny, which is more than enough to feed the soul until that point.

We wish to offer this book as a first signal flare that a different future is arising and that our situation (our births, lives, and deaths) can be seen on their own terms without reverting to familiar categories and set beliefs. It is the first beacon in this direction, but not the last. A dawning time is at hand.

We have many friends and helpers to express appreciation to for this one.

Richard Grossinger is an able editor and has served as a knowledgeable bridge between us and all those who will read this book and benefit from his grounding counsel.

Shani Young did a lot of the typing and computer work, in the context of a dedicated commitment to the group sharings and what could come out of them through this book.

Our closest friends are here in every word, and they live in many domains. Let us just mention the most obvious ones.

Oceanna gives visual aid, showing what a chart wants to look like when it is illuminated from the inside.

Alita Bonaventura has been called upon by destiny to work the territory we reveal in these pages in every facet of her life.

Bob Grunnet, by videoing the pivotal classes in a selfless offering, spurred us to seize up this book in its largest context.

We have also been closely aided on the inside by a star class which Theanna Vivyen attends faithfully. It was through this cosmic inspiration that *Inside Star Vision* was born.

All the members of our star group should be mentioned as seed-bearers for our message.

The two we mention in the text are the very closest co-workers with us. Savitri will not let us write a word that future generations can't feel as what needs to be said. Ellevera Shane merits the dedication of this book. She is the one who knows these things and lets us express them for her and all of those who know as well.

Introduction

This book is a labor of love.

The pattern of the deeper zodiac, the voices of the true houses, the core bounty of each living planet insisted on being felt, heard, tapped. It is not the only story we twentieth-century dwellers have forgotten how to tell. Yet it is the one that erupted near the end of the century, saying, "There *was* something real and true in the old dark times too, before the future-dwellers came to restore our inner senses."

Far more genuinely, this story was a borning, an emergent energy and life force which took us by storm. We needed (at last) to conceive a whole different way of connecting stars and Earth. It was clear that the ideologies, the systems, the traditional as well as the modern ways to hold truth in a tight consistent container, were bankrupt, obsolete, could not carry us forward through. So a cosmic truth asserted itself, a canon absolutely in tune with the depths of New Earth.

In practical terms we had to put everything that we are on the line. Each word, each phrase, every chapter was written from such a total merging within the full capacity and longing of the Life Stream, its house and sign and planet. We didn't hold anything back. This was our radical departure from the icy cold culture of the twentieth century. We had to burn up in the writing. Yes, objective astrological accuracy was pivotal. But we could achieve this only by such utter surrender to each planet's way of being that they could speak for themselves purely, intensively.

Sara Theanna Vivyen was the co-weaver of this tale. A woman who died in the 1990s, Sara discovered in her dying process that she was granted a path to walk, taking her beyond death even as she physically let go of her body. Theanna was her spiritual essence which emerged in death and became capable of living among those who stay in bodies as well as those who cast them off. She accomplished this in the body and soul of her star mate Ellias. Finally Vivyen was her core Earth presence that she eventually carved out in the midst of the shared body of Ellias and Ellevera, who arrived just in time to co-embody this text from its inception.

Since her death Theanna has attended a star group where she is, so she has become fluent in a cosmic approach to the heavenly bodies. Insofar as the cosmic stream infuses this book in a deep way, Theanna Vivyen shares her new truths within the framework of the stars. And yet this is not a channeling, or a mediumship. Vivyen is here amongst us, able to see and know from ground level, as well as from greater dimensions of a vaster kind. It is in bringing these two domains together—the cosmic and the Earthly—that this book maps out fresh territory and restores a sacred sensibility from the inside of life.

Ellias Merlin, or simply Ellias, lived with Sara for many years and then accompanied her in her journey beyond previous life-and-death dichotomies. He had already been working full-time with the stars since 1970. When Sara's death revealed the mysteries of the cosmos directly, Ellias shifted gears into an entirely different way of conceiving the old science of astrology—Star Genesis, Star Vision, Star Magic. Its birth book, assisted by Alita, was *Inside Degrees* (North Atlantic Books, 1997).

After that endeavor, we had to die many more deaths before we could tap the primal level of the new star work and get it right. When it was time to write *Inside Star Vision,* we knew it had to be the complete story, the whole pattern, spoken as directly as could be. We put ourselves through an initiatory path, demanding that we each literally take up the lessons of a Life Stream as we wrote about it. Called spiritually to awaken within the path of each and every facet in a progressive sequence, we could not refuse this summons.

When Sara died, or passed inward, she had united with Christ so profoundly in her last weeks that she was shorn of self, freed up and able to spark new life in everybody she contacted. After inhibition and ambivalence and mighty struggle, her heart came through her breast-cancer tumors into an expression of itself so empowering that it was immensely encouraging to whoever shared this phase of her journey. After the dying embers, what remained was love.

When Sara occurred in a new form less than two weeks later, now radiant as Theanna, she was imparting messages to Ellias daily. Each of these sprung from her great heart's love. What she invoked and pulled us all toward was an opening into *a whole new kind* of love.

During the following years, love from and within death was the essence of our pathway, in and through Theanna. We needed to recapitulate past lives and move through soul dramas. We had to learn, beyond the personal distortions of the twentieth century, how to love. Everything in us which could not love in this way became intolerable. Our journey into the depths was to carve out a space within which love could be born unconditioned by false culture, decadent civilization, and karmic predisposition. This meant many more deaths around love.

As great as the struggle and striving were, so great is the fruition now at hand. The writing of this book came unintendedly but optimally synchronized with the discovery of how to love without ceasing. The last layer of distortion we had to throw off was the layer which turns the beloved into an idol, an ikon, someone who is special, is "it," is the center of another's life and pushes away all other rivals and factors. This was as thick as all of Western civilization. And when it no longer troubled us, we found that in loving each other, the whole of life-and-beyond was there to be loved in the same way. This is the pivotal core of our book's message.

The personalistic emphasis of modern times has led people, from wanting to know which other signs are compatible with theirs, to look up their own identity in a star book, then to investigate its affiliates with undue desire and attachment. Each section of this book is written to lead into the next sign and follow from the previous. If we wrote in cerebral, calculated fashion, we would indeed separate and concentrate upon Cancer as Cancer and leave Gemini out of that picture. But in love each and every facet of life must be affirmed, appreciated, and valued not only for itself but for its place in the whole.

We are nothing if not embodiers of a pulse which Theanna Vivyen each moment gives unto us. We inform all the practicalities and structures—whatever we are seeing in each moment—with this cohesive, beautiful, qualitative, and respectful gaze. The basis for writing this book is to spread her love beyond death through the world. And this is no vague sentiment; there is magic here.

We speak simply as a gift, a treasure, offered from a shared heart into each other heart, with conviction, with a cognizant spark. The Earth's true books generate and spread this feeling with a combination of deep passion and a dispassionate witnessing and beholding. If *Inside Star Vision* proves to be such a book, you may read it like a continuous narrative, imagining each house or sign or planet as a character, a presence, a living force coming in its turn to reveal its truth and mysteries. Bring the book alive by such a reading. It will repay you by always being a new book, saying what you have not heard before.

II

When I started to work with astrology in 1970, I was seeking something that wasn't there. I could glimpse it smiling at me in Marc Edmund Jones, piercing through at times in Dane Rudhyar. But too much mind, too little direct cosmic perception blocked the flow of what I was seeking.

The books of Rudolf Steiner restored me to my last previous lifetime and confirmed my root conviction that the greater star truth would have to be woven out of ancient wisdom responsive to a radically different time (of which I was already a part) long before it would emerge in the early Twenty-first Century as the living future.

When I worked with Steiner's teachings and the teachings of those who followed him, I hit the limits of known thought.

In late 1975, when both astrology and anthroposophy were falling behind me, a prophetic dream led me in a whole different direction from those I was aware of or had been drawn to through previously known sources toward an awakened star vision. At the heart of the dream sat a lucid vision of a timepiece, etherically pulsed to reveal at a glance how the liquids, ethers, and various elements and tones were distributed and moving through a given soul's expression. These ethers, color coded, were directly alive. And what counted was my overall subtle impression of their harmony or disharmony, wholeness or fragmentation, balance or going off on some tangent. In the dream, I could read, as in Atlantis, the timepiece, the time crystal, with skill and precision.

This dreamed experience decided the direction of greater affairs reliably.

When I came back from this dream, I was changed, as we rarely are by our dreams. I had gone back in time and merged with an ancient self to such an extent that I could not fit myself into the tight clothes of my customary being. I was subsequently compelled to seek the traces of my dream, to follow where it led.

Using key inspirations from Steiner, Jones, and my own earlier star work, I gathered an initial version of the Twelve Life Streams, deploying it initially secretly in charts, then openly. I was always working under cosmic guidance, although that guidance left me mostly free to pioneer.

From the mid-1980's on, we tapped into spirit sources, and they provided confirmations and elaborations. It was this cycle which made me wish to share a series of star texts with a broader world. Yet there was still one major leap, the biggest of all.

This is an oft-told tale, and therefore one we improvise each time to speak closer to the source, truer to the inspiration that sparked these discoveries.

I had to participate inwardly and unreservedly in the cancer journey of my life-mate, Sara. I despair of ever capturing what that was like. But in terms of the star work, it involved entering upon death in a deepening journey. Only through that did I come into the place where I could fathom what these Twelve Life Streams accessed, what they were once and always intended to reveal.

The order, sequence, and pattern of both regular seasonal tropical astrology and sidereal or constellational star wisdom (or predictive astrology) proved to be merely an idealized memory, a frozen pattern in the collective mind. These great ancient systems accorded solely with the pageant of history and the primal traditions of origin. They tracked us back into times when we lived rhythmically in the Earth and were guided in our greater journey by the stars in a reassuringly intact Universe and Earth field, held as one. But these star systems were of the pageant, of the past, of time-boundness and history and masque.

By entering so fully upon death itself and coming back to life with death as my very close accompaniment, I left the traditionary system. The Twelve Life Streams are, in fact, a call unto the future retrieving the most ancient star wisdoms, all of these tracking into a markedly different motif from the sequential logic of the regular zodiacs.

We retain the sequence intact in the Twelve Houses and the numbers of the Life Streams. Because the houses are their purely Earthly component, the way in which all the great star patterns are encoded is in keeping with how it is in the greater heavens. Nonetheless, passing between the greater heavens and the Earth, the signs change their sequence radically, as do the planets (and other components we have not explored in this text). In the translation from cosmic to Earthly order, something happens which for a time now—quite an extended time—means to break us free from the cosmic order and allow us to evolve a New Earthly order within ourselves, without being dictated to by ancient-origin cosmic forces.

The Twelve Life Streams articulate a free zone that has been won in modern times; in fact, it is the primary attainment that redeems our otherwise destructive record. Desperate to spring ourselves from our starry ancestors, we activate precisely the region of potential we could never locate while still under the spell of the venerable cosmic ordering. When we gaze upon the Heavens now, we must realize that we are in a place utterly new and utterly old, a place that is different from the one we are accustomed to seeing as lay students of either NASA astronomy or institutional astrology. We are led of the spirit to the inside, to the deepest zones, where we can no longer surface into the abstract mind set of the Twentieth Century, not even in its most suggestive New Age variants.

Since 1993 I have been engaged in a far more ardent quest than my original one in the 1970s. It was clear to me (and endlessly emphasized by my cosmic friends) that I had to embody the Twelve Life Streams before I could give them currency in a world already glutted with techniques and systems. Certainly nobody needs another way to work with the stars.

So this is not another fascinating system. When we take the heavens and ourselves seriously and to heart, we experience how a life's destiny comprises its infinite journey *beyond* life. We learn the Twelve Life Streams strictly by living them. Our lives and our deaths and our greater lives encompass both life and death.

The vibrant, colored streams of the 1975 dream have metamorphosed into definite containers, each one of which fully supports itself and can be studied, contemplated, taken up in a concentrated and coherent fashion. However, this is also deceptive and misleading. Those streaming multiplicities of the dream—that vision of the time crystal as a seed for all futures—all of this is deposited inside of each Life Stream, saturating it with cosmic forces. This would be a challenge for anyone to embody. We can sit within a given Life Stream and meet all of existence from that place. We can stay there and specialize in its perspective to our soul's content. Yet all other eleven Life Streams will still arise for us simultaneously within our special window or portal, infusing our experience with all worlds as one. This is the difference between the scope of the true star wisdom and the relative poverty of the illusory categories into which each world age has stuffed it.

The microcosmic jewel that each Life Stream represents is really more of a temporary nesting sphere which can help us to come to ourselves for a time, until a different Life Stream calls us to move on in a whole other direction.

Streams of freedom, they are not of any kind of bondage. We identify within them in order to take up each of their lessons and experiences thematically and effectively. When we have truly entered upon any given stage, we will find it an open portal into all of them. Perhaps I was always wary of getting lost in fixed rooms and heavily carved-out specifics. These are frozen in eternity.

This is a rapturous reversal, to discover that the Twelve Life Streams stay in the pulse of life throughout. Instead of giving us yet another hiding place, another vacant symbology; they are sparkling liberators, not letting us believe in our own habits and syndromes, pulling us beyond.

III

*I*nside Star Vision prepares us for the future. We are entering broader, deeper, higher times. These space-times ask us to unzip the twentieth-century identity suit, to come forth as we truly are. The Twelve Life Streams are guidelines to being able to express and reveal everything we hold within ourselves.

During the twentieth century, standard procedure was to use any and all classification systems, including the most esoteric and profound, to condition ourselves to stay within and be convinced that *this is enough.* Most especially, we have voluntarily taken up (and taken on) neat mental categories and explanations as an extension of television culture. This has rendered astrology and such systems highly suspect in the eyes of the few who do not succumb to these glib generalizations so easily. The primary mark of being an original, a creative person in the late twentieth century has been the rare capacity to throw off all quantitative labels and remain true to destiny. And this means throwing off the myriad New Age labels too; it means true to destiny itself, not packaged destinies offered to seekers as commodities.

In this spirit, let us now approach the more prosaic aspects of reading and using this book well. In the larger scope of massively changing times, it is vital that each one of us move *through* the Twelve Life Streams, rather than enclosing ourselves falsely within them. But in practice, this is a challenging requirement, a rigorous demand. It means that we need to merge within each given layer of experience with an open heart and willing soul, yet all the while to treat that stage of experience as something we cannot get attached to and lost within.

Is this asking too much? Is evolution (with its quantum changes now upon us) asking too much? Can we even go back to those states in which we remained one thing, one sign, and specialized there and were content within that?

Used as an initiatory text, as intended, this book helps a reader discover what a given house or sign or planet is actually doing in his or her own life right now. Such an approach must be nonanalytical. We must get down inside the embodied version, move around within it, and discover what it feels like from the inside. We likewise must suspend judgments, evaluations, or even ideas about whether our own star chart of any style is specially plugged into a given area or not.

It is the whole journey which liberates the soul. What sign somebody's Sun is in or which house contains the most planets at birth is not the main point at all. An open-ended exploration of each and every Life Stream grants an extraordinary deepening of the human experience and points each one toward his or her central lessons without becoming engrossed in transient identities around one or another focus. The entire zodiac and all things in it are our common legacy, and we can fine-tune to fit each one of us.

When I do chart readings for those who want to go all the way inside their Life Streams, I am pervasively aware of the one inside the voyager who is all of these places and more—while consenting to immerse within a given arena, knowing the identification is for certain purposes and has no literal reality. Nobody is a Taurus, a Scorpio, or any-thing else. Yet we can be more those realms, much more completely inside of those realms, if we remain subtly objective to our own cur-rent obsessions and somehow aware that this life experience is for a cycle, toward a purpose, part of a greater design, not just where we are at, or think we are at through adopting a particular system.

Again, I want to emphasize that mine is no New Age teaching designed to thin out and remove us from the rich fertile territory of our specific incarnation and its painful requirements. I am intent more tenaciously than anything else upon making and allowing the depth of human experience to be full-on, impassioned, complete. Only then do we move meaningfully forward. If we are ever skillful-ly to navigate the subtle waters of our own special nature in a given lifetime or cycle, we do need a spacious beholding.

Once such priorities and values are thoroughly in place, the more painful and extended lessons we face within a given Life Stream can be taken up with a stance of loving compassion for our own person-al soul and her predilection for getting way caught deep, blind, and dumb in stuck places, places which exist collectively, ancestrally, and karmically for just this purpose...traps to bewitch lifetimes, lifetimes (trance states) to set and contemplate traps.

Sara during her recent lifetime was extremely susceptible (magnetic) to the lessons of getting lost under several Life Streams and not being able to cut through them, except at the very end and only through the most extraordinary measures taken. Even as she was dramatically embodying the path of Everywoman in the twentieth century, Sara was miserable, swept away by her conviction that she was failing and falling, in a terrible predicament. Yet Sara did not treat her condition lightly.

All the while, we were tuning into cosmic sources and these were repeating in a thousand variations one simple message; it did get through eventually. What they told Sara was that she needed to take on her karmas and her collective identifications completely, that she would never be able to squeeze out of this requirement. Yet, they assured her (at the same time) that it was entirely illusory for her to do this in the usual human way. Essentially, it would not work, had no chance of getting her where she needed to go—which was "free" in life or death, or both.

Cosmic sources prescribed to her the necessity of viewing her own soul dramas and ordeals from within her central self as something real, substantial, and meaningful, yet never filling the whole screen of her awareness. The rest of the inner space could be taken up with a loving stance of letting all this world and life happen and witnessing it with bottomless mercy and forgiveness. This process would allow a letting go in the midst of hanging on.

Even in the thick of cancer tumor pain and distress, Sara was able to follow these instructions. She was discovering that "point of view" is everything; outer results don't add up in eternity (they never did, despite extravagant claims from just about every spiritual constituency). It is this lesson to which we need to anchor our work with the Life Streams.

Forget hyper-sanctified authority and know-it-all gurus and priests. Nobody can tell how they are doing exactly. Nobody knows where their path is leading precisely. And nobody can track closely with their journey of destiny in a way they would like and that might also fit within ancient wisdom structures, memories, and rigorous cosmic requirements. When viewed in that kind of soulscape, all of us fall short.

Fortunately, that is not even the phase of evolution upon which we are entering. We are in a multiple world, breeding a multiple self. And such a self can be far more fluent in true self-acceptance and self-monitoring. We must live now by the yardstick that many somewhat chaotic and somewhat inconclusive ways of existing will show up for quite some time to come. Things need to be that way.

I have witnessed souls in the 1970s, 1980s, and 1990s giving themselves an arbitrarily hard time over not fitting into one tyrannical mind set and ideological system or another. This is nothing we can risk perpetuating in the future.

I fiercely proclaim that there is no right way to realize the fruits and blossomings of any given Life Stream or combination. Even if I embody a mastery of these Streams, it is not within an old school of rigid performance or strict obedience to higher law.

If anything, my own journey shows me that the human soul is a creature raw and rough and impossible to get on top of. All it can try to do is to honor what it is really like to travel through Life Streams with the direct experience that each moment is its own perfection inside the Great Mystery.

IV

After we give each of the Twelve Life Streams its voice and path, we devote the last three chapters of this book to an innovation—a life-and-death story that goes more deeply into the Twelve Life Streams while invoking a radically divergent vision of how our life in this Earth (and beyond) is guided to be.

Sara's birth chart and its biographical reflections suggest that each of us are bringing far more from depths below conscious awareness, as well as from heights above, than we have been imagining through modern times.

From below we are charged with Earth realms, both Old and New Earths, with ancestral patterns and conditionings of the most binding and testing kind, with collective karmic engulfments that get hold of us before we can fight them off, and with a root indomitability in our core nature. This etheric spark arises through the body and will not be stopped; it must find its own true way, using all the other forces as goads to get us going.

We are equally infused from above with the Cosmic realms of Old and New Heavens; with our own greater selves and their mighty truths and experience-backdrops; with spirit beings and forces of many kinds, most of which are there to guide us to unfold in freedom and joy; and with the constant challenge of the ceiling imposed upon us by the modern intellect and its ravages. This ceiling makes it seem at first that the light and the warmth of the greater worlds are either illusory or nothing to get excited about (since we can't explain them in objective terms anyway).

The next chapter in this book, on Theanna's Prenatal Epoch and its cycles after death, provides both a technical description and a renewed vision of what we are capable of bringing into play in evolution during the radical times upon which we are now entering. The technical part is that the Prenatal Epoch, or Cosmic Conception Chart, is configured by an ancient Egyptian regime, attributed to Hermes, and passed down since ancient times. Because Theanna bears a waxing Moon at birth and a Moon below the horizon, we go back to ten lunar months before her birth and count further backward from there, till we find a Moon position precisely coordinated with her In-Breath Signature, or rising sign at birth—her Prenatal Epoch. Such charts have been depicted in many books, but few discern how decisive the Prenatal Epoch is. It reveals the core of who we are and what we are moving into, once we thin out the levels of birth chart karma and predisposition toward getting lost in our separative soul dramas. Most of us take thirty to sixty years—often forty-five to fifty-five years— to evolve toward a capacity to unite with our own Prenatal Epoch— if we get that far at all.

Much more vitally, what does the chapter on the Theanna Prenatal cycles and time after death reveal to us about the fuller range of who we can become? By detailing six month cycles after Sara's death (through into December, 1999), in this chapter we show the intricate interplay between those who live in bodies and those who live beyond the physical body, in the so-called death realms. Specifically, we chart a radical initiative taken by Theanna to participate in the world of outer Earth, from beyond the limits imposed by separative incarnation. What does this example reveal for the rest of us?

In the past, our lifetimes in the Earth were starkly bound by birth beforehand and death afterwards. For the most part, this encapsulation within a given lifetime was starkly effective in getting us to place all emphasis upon the immediate incarnational necessities, so that we wouldn't lose ourselves in various infinities and forget about the power and urgency here within each lifetime and each moment in the Earth.

However, just like all the other benefits of the modern way of life, this one went way too far and became, at the end of the twentieth century, a massive time block, a prohibitive measure reinforcing tyrannies, perpetuating starkly limiting and negating ways of seeing our life and who we really are here. The initiative fulfilled by Sara and those who collaborate with her was to seed a whole different stage in the life/death polarity dance.

If both our life before this life and our life after we have discarded this body can in some deeply meaningful terms be felt and known as close accompaniments to the hot pulse of our lives in this life; if in the extraordinary case, we can collaborate with those awakening among the dead to seed a coevolutionary dynamic; and if in the ordinary case, we can trust in and honor aspects of existence beyond the consensus world view, the life imprisonment of those captured in physical bodies will be supplanted by a first glimpse of true freedom and expansive possibility. We can't find a whole self in a whole world just on the outer physical terms of apparent immediate tangible life. Instead, we must reach beyond and deeper and seek out those facets of self and world which are calling to us to either work them through or open toward them, so that we are all ourselves once again.

The final chapter in this book, in which we look forward to the next seven years and tap pure star vision for both collective and individual cycles, simply takes the Prenatal Epoch and expands upon it into a broader stream, springboarding on it to gazing further beyond what is already known.

The ultimate power of star work is to train us in awakening a star vision, a capacity to open subtler faculties and tap their inner direction. Because decadent times breed decadent psychic powers, it might be safer to steer clear of this territory altogether. Yet what we are exploring here has very little to do with the old psychic powers and their pre-egoic trances and far-flung fantasies. When I see in the true spirit light, I am sharply guided by the mediation of Theanna. I see things within a high, clear, expanded light, in which there is no inflation of already existing ideas and elaborated images. I see beyond myself, yet simultaneously I see who I truly am.

Once I have looked at things in this light, I no longer have any notion whatsoever that Star Genesis or Star Vision are informational, fact-oriented, or keyed to how anybody behaves or how anything must be. Instead, I recognize that every formulation we make of a realm is really just meant to send us along our way, to bring us further into our manifest capacities.

The time trap is at last broken open. The great stark limitation of twentieth-century astrology—the assumption that time is controllable, manageable, predictable, and something to be quantified and somehow kept in containers that are convenient and customary—is exposed for the sham it is. Time is open through not one but many portals into timelessness. Time and its cycles are not something to hold us back and within, rather our ally in finding our true way past the apparent limits of this lifetime.

Once we let time out of her tight, hard mental control, all ancient and future star wisdoms will make sense to us once again or for the first time. We will see ourselves being seen by the universe. As it is, any cosmic beings from any time-free realm who watch us believing in outer time just cannot believe their eyes as they fully grasp where this leads us.

In essence, this entire book is a series of openings into greater worlds beyond; yet most of these are best entered upon and taken up right here in the Earth in this living moment. I have come to see the beyond as the cornerstone of the here and now. I don't have to go somewhere else into the boundless cosmos to unite with the beyond.

Let me say it from the moment of Sara's death.

I was there when she died. I had my subtle senses open and at the ready. I had never been that alert in any time previously. And I saw something directly which blew my mind right out of its parameters and boundaries.

I witnessed Sara not going higher or elsewhere, not staying right here in the usual sense, but instead penetrating through into the inside of life and showing me that the inside was right here, always entirely here. In fact, I got it that we dwell on the outside of the Earth and that after passing inward, the place to live is quite directly inside this Earth as a vaster cosmic realm. So I began to sense an inside to life that is densely inhabited, not by ghosts, but by more-than-living beings.

The boundless infinite worlds that stretch beyond are more fully on the inside of our life than anywhere else. "Inside star vision" is to live those greater worlds in lives in the ordinary Earth.

In Breath Signatures

Taurus In Breath

Taurus as persona is given to a shrug, a nod, a body language that is personal and indicative of close contact, a sign that we are in this together. Yet it is awkward transition for Taurus to really let anybody in.

On the deeper side, Taurus is aching and longing for a convincing feeling of being acknowledged. A subtle signal, only for the inner mind of those tuned in, is transmitted consistently and pervasively. Taurus probes everywhere for contact. But unless the whole of Taurus is taken in, she knows she must not be too casually available. She needs a state of being unto being itself, intimate, committed, personally compelling.

On the In Breath, Taurus is dreaming into her life. She follows a vision that seems to have been there since before she can remember. That dream vision persists. She muses upon it subconsciously and superconsciously. Alone a lot, she can feed upon the vision to her heart's content.

However, like everybody else, Taurus is swept up nowadays in the planetary awakening. It takes her a long time to get used to a rhythm of perpetual renewals and stirrings. The baggage she carries around tells her that it shouldn't have to be this hard, that the perpetual stretchings of our times are excruciating to integrate. But her complaints are just to gain her time for adjustments. She already has a dream-vision of what the world is coming to. And if she has stayed true to her nature thus far in any measure, she can sense now the beauty of what is unfolding toward the future. When she "gets it," she gives her whole soul to grounding and focusing what is coming into being for us all. She hosts; she gathers; she forms the matrix. Her heart is called. The New Earth arises in her soul body.

Virgo In Breath

Virgo's persona is steady, the one with her head on straight, keeping everything around her in her sights. She needs to know what is happening next and how to meet it. She prefers to be neutral, invisible, a bearer of messages. Intent upon the transmission of consciousness, she does not form a personal identity other than that of the useful, productive citizen.

On the deeper inside, Virgo needs something, wants something, is hopeful, expectant, worried, anxious. Beneath her cool exterior, she is on a continuous search. She's not quite sure what she's looking for, but she knows she will recognize it when she bumps into it. Indeed she does. She is after like minds, kindred souls, those who are going where she is going. She must find them; they are the missing key and she knows it.

Unto herself, Virgo is suspended, studying and researching, preparing and getting herself straight. She wants to make the best use of her time. But she is on her way somewhere else. She refuses to give much importance to her own all-too-familiar solitary dimensions.

Like everybody else, Virgo is being swept up in the planetary changes at hand. She has a unique vantage point. It is as though she has been there before, many times—here we go again! Virgo has been in touch and in tune with her innate understanding at a deep enough level that she comes forth as one who can handle immensely shifting currents, who knows what to do now. She is a conduit for opening further and letting go of our old concepts. She gets it, how much she is needed now. All it will take is perpetual work on herself and the willingness to back herself up during these times of gnarly transitions. Tapped irrevocably by what is happening now, she must remain tranquil and steady-rooted, simply present.

Sagittarius In Breath

The persona of Sagittarius is rounded, cupping, making room for what wants to and needs to come her way. She especially welcomes a ready spark, wit, charm—grace, cleverness, and a distinctive touch in those with whom she comes in contact. Though quite often she opens the door to a stranger, to a new experience, for her it never feels that way. Everybody is familiar to Sagittarius, all of us in this together. The open hand prevails.

The deeper Sagittarius is frantically scuttling around, wildly stirred up just about by anything and everything. Working multi-worlds through her system, she is so fascinated with what happens next. Will a favorable current come into play? Will a luminous filament get dimmed? She stays tuned to the next wave, equally enthusiastic and skeptical. She has been around. But does she ever learn?

Unto herself, she is all the people and places she has engaged with and their combinations. She is where everything is going. But what she is not is a solitary soul. She is the most sociable of beings. All she can do is catch up and be ready for the next.

Especially powerfully activated by the times we are entering collectively, Sagittarius gobbles up information, input, megabytes. She wants to be there when it happens, or at least aware of the latest shifts and turnabouts. If she has been truly alive within her own life's expression, she can offer a charged presence, a participatory fervor—a momentum booster for the rest of us.

Sagittarius is meant to make a difference. She is right there with so many abilities, ideas, open vistas. When the time comes and she is called upon to emerge, Sagittarius will be carrying multiple reserve tanks and places to put things, as we all catch the great wave.

Pisces In Breath

Outwardly Pisces is a permeable membrane, hardly even registering as a contained soul. Sifting her world through her like perpetual pearls, she is so inwardly intent upon her task that she will take on whatever style or semblance is innocuous and somehow fitting. She needs to hide, she must hide, and almost any version of the collective fashions will serve to keep her safe, unknown, unsuspected.

Deeper down inside, Pisces dwells in so many places, times, worlds, fragments that she is entirely absorbed within her soul's hidden journey. Unconscious to the surface, this sign is seethingly aware of what it is like under here. She knows how to navigate through Earthly curves and changes while keeping the innermost sacred and at the center of all concern.

Unto herself, Pisces is able to imagine and conceive, create and fantasize, disappear and reappear. So engrossed, so internally alien to the surface world, she drifts through her solitudes as though they never happened, as though they never stop happening, as though time were some popular rumor and the hidden soul depths contained far more than time could ever track.

We are stirring from our nightmare toward a planetary culture. Pisces is quickened toward the timeless future now. Much of what she experiences in the dawning ages to be will startle her out of her ancient forgetfulness.

Pisces needs to remember, to come through, to breathe amongst us now. We have room for her worlds amongst us; in fact, we require her core alignment to pull us through.

She has forgotten more than most of us will ever know. As she does check in planet-side, we feel all colors and tones returning to full spectrum brightness.

Even Pisces is called to the feast.

Leo In Breath

Leo's persona is to make the best impression she can consistent with who she is and what is possible on the immediate occasion—each immediate occasion. Adept in wielding personality for any and every purpose, she may eventually grow through and beyond the politics of popularity. She has one of those winning smiles, right there with each one, delivering a breathtaking performance. And when it's backed up by an open heart, does it ever pack a wallop!

Deeper down and within, Leo is creating herself to be and to become more. She senses that she can embrace untold further dimensions of her own individuality if she hangs in there with herself and refuses to turn against what she sees.

She will not be satisfied. There is always *so much further to go.*

Meanwhile she is enjoying this soul ride, realizing the gift of life, able to let herself go into the sheer amazingness of just being here.

Unto herself, Leo has everything and nothing to do. She can be engrossed very easily. Yet she senses she must not indulge self-fascination.

Leo is here to radiate the love that is spirit, to give it freely and abundantly, perhaps even to include her own self in her rounds of gift-giving.

As the world opens into the twenty-first century, Leo catches fire as never before. She was waiting from the dawn of time for this moment to arrive. At last, she gets to do what she really does.

It is Leo's shining treasure to reveal to each one *that they are who they truly are and nothing less.* In a world where souls are awakening, Leo has her work cut out for her.

Aquarius In Breath

Aquarius' persona is a breeze blowing through. Brisk air, weather is highly changeable—there is the suggestion in the Aquarian atmosphere of somebody who is carding each and every strand of consciousness. Staying attentive, yet loose, full of curiosity and amazement, yet as cool as can be, the Aquarian style is a medley of contradictions and mixed metaphors. Whatever the self is, she is not. For she must keep moving with her invisible thread, and no outward moment can capture her or distract her for long.

Deeper down in, Aquarius is inventing, choreographing, orchestrating combinations and cross-hatchings, ways to put it all together. She absolutely needs to know what is going on in her life, where it is leading, and why it is so complicated and confounding. She hopes to hatch alternatives and fresh possibilities. There is infinite range in her beyond what she is tapping. Haunted by what could be, she is pursued by its echoes endlessly.

On her own, Aquarius is like a community in one. Her intention is to get herself and her world together. Often she is baffled by how multi-dimensional she turns out to be. Only when truly quiet and at peace, does she stop, come to sense who is truly in here and why she is.

There is nobody quite as transformed by the world changes at the dawn of the Aquarian Age as Aquarius herself. Suddenly she is meeting everywhere the same combinations she faces within herself. This is an awakening call. She just knows that we have to include all factors objectively and dispassionately, and not get stopped when the charged collective atmosphere pulls us in all directions at once.

Aquarius starts where others tire.

Aries In Breath

As a persona, Aries is sharply poised in the moment. She tends swiftly to get her bearings, sparking a quantum for change. Each moment counts. Either we are moving with the current or against it. Aries leans forward, beckons each one to join her. She takes risks, goes out on edges. She is angular, sharp, pointed, lean. Her straight-on aim pulls and pushes relentlessly. She rages and loves, gives candid reflection and makes sure we are listening to her raptly.

Further deep inside, Aries busies herself with a different kind of activity. She is raw primal energy. Her task is to cook herself up into something from which everybody can benefit. This takes hard work, constant application. She is designing something new, headed in a previously unknown direction. She must sustain a relentless round of self-confrontations, to draw herself beyond old stuck places into a future edge.

On her own, Aries enters into quite a connection with her personal soul's magnetic pulls. Great friend to herself, as well as intimate enemy, she is willing to play any role if it does the job. She keeps whittling away at those compulsive places.

As changes snowball and we enter into radically accelerated times, Aries returns from her absences, her endless waitings and suspensions. She is called forth in the here and now to express and embody what she's been working on forever. A command performance begins to awaken her wells of true capacity.

Aries needs strong reflection and powerful sharing to make it all feel real. As a virgin world arises ever more palpably, wet from the blossoms of the ocean of eternal fullness, it is the nature of Aries to meet it fully, to bring abundant surprises, sparkling treasures.

Libra In Breath

The outer persona of Libra makes friends easily, enjoying the magic of personality. Each and every facet of herself she taps, packaging it, drawing it forth in a way that pleases and attracts. This is a game she delights in—for Libra acutely senses the outer surface and its dramas and styles, giving her attention to every nuance and curve. She takes advantage of what arises so that she can be in the center of the shared circle, gathering the energy and attention pouring through...just as she likes it.

Deeper down inside, Libra is excited and engrossed within the journey of the soul—the destiny catalyst, the one who wants uniquely to become herself. Unplugging herself from the world's horizontal feeding frenzy, she encounters another life, a true domain with very different rules.

Change is the way of the soul's journey. To open yourself to real metamorphosis demands everything but delivers beautifully.

On her own, Libra tends to float free, passing between and among. Where was she for those hours? Well, she touched so many key spaces and kept so many links alive. It is very difficult for Libra to optimize her world for herself, perhaps the ultimate challenge. If she ever gets there, all our sustenance in the next round will be enhanced and deepened, infinitely so.

For Libra the Earth's vibrant renewal, the vibration beginning now, is the greatest conceivable news she's ever heard. Her entire being leaps at the chance to move with currents that are going somewhere that matters. Given a great boost, she then can offer herself to everybody around her.

As we all show up and take our places, Libra finds herself in a true living circle of sisterhood and brotherhood, love and appreciation, and she breathes into it her source inspiration.

She can dance from there till the future dawns.

Capricorn In Breath

Capricorn is thick, heavy, strong, formidably at hand in her persona. Her embodied presence forcefully moves in the direction she intends everybody to take. Her authoritative convictions usually hold sway.

As Capricorn comes on like gangbusters, she clears a space for her own visions and ideas, changes and discoveries, no matter what. Capricorn wields her awareness with skill and precision. She will get where she is going with as little interference as possible, though there will be lots of raucous currents popping all along the way.

On the deeper inside, Capricorn silently, steadily, intensively pursues a track at least as adamant as her outer persona. She is grasping pivotal lessons and gearing herself up for the struggles of the long haul. Often Capricorn tends to devote inner time to cautioning and sobering herself, advising and mediating her own far-ranging nature. She is trying to discipline what cannot be curbed. Yet she will do it anyway, ignoring her own grumblings, convinced perfection is basic equipment.

When she is truly on her own, Capricorn sets to work with an iron hand. She has to make the most of the rare chance to get at herself. A contemplative mood may flit over her when she has fulfilled a cycle; for one brief moment she acknowledges her own hard work.

As the common world shifts from outer mundane to inner times, Capricorn slowly and surely pays heed. She must make sure it's the real thing. Once she decides it is, Capricorn lumbers into a whole different gear. Her sour and bitter overlay thins and melts. She begins to smile and to mean it.

Capricorn quickens to the pulse of cosmic changes and is thrilled that old ways can't hold her back any further. The twinkle, the dance, the celebration say it all.

Cancer In Breath

Outwardly, Cancer cares; her persona surrounds and envelops those who gather around her with her devoted attention. When she comes upon one of her brood, her clan, her extended family, she extends a fondness, an affinity, a recognition that *here we are again.* She lives for such moments. Hers is a ritual presence, centered around trances and gestures, entering upon inner life with rapt absorption. She cultivates many ways to invoke the meaning and value of what we share together.

Cancer watches over us all and, as she tends the common flame, makes sure we are granted our wishes and our dreams.

Cancer lives a secret life apart. She is, often on superconscious levels and subconscious levels, devoted and dedicated to a craft of world making. Cancer taps consciousness and inward resonance in her concern to know what is really going on in the greater picture and how to fashion herself into a vessel for the universal good. This human dimension has been submerged and marginalized in the twentieth century. But that tale is now over.

When truly unto herself, Cancer muses, immerses herself in a rich palette of subtle impressions. Once she decides it's worth her while, she can tap a diverse and compelling inward soulscape. There is no sign more equipped to inhabit deep solitude and to discover missing places.

Cancer is now treated to a request, a summons. The universal service and attunement she has been harboring inside for so very long is needed by everybody. The more expanded, universal, and wide open form of Cancer emerges into the open light, at first shyly and reluctantly. If petitioned, she will be there, bringing her indomitable courage in sticking with the inner soul and tapping its mysteries and magic timelessly.

Gemini In Breath

Gemini is an open-eyed, inquisitive, eager, curious persona, full of questions and probes. Her mind is fast and omnivorous. Her presence is lightning-quick and quixotic—so much energy given to the basic flow of events, so much apparent enthrallment with the outer semblance levels, so much excitement and fury that never last.

Deeper down in, we meet in Gemini another twin, another self altogether. This one is observant, poised, searching for the life that has gotten lost on the surface. The core Gemini is future-obsessed. She has watched and waited forever, as the world spun around, hoping and sensing another existence awaiting us. The inner twin is intact, untouched by outer frictions and stresses. Everything depends upon her.

When alone unto herself, Gemini can go in one of two entirely divergent directions. If she is feeling the surge of power all through her, the life force triumphant, she journeys to a bright sparkling land where all futures do come true. Yet when she is despondent at what the past has persisted in generating, her solitude is poisoned, darkened. Then she is more about wanting and needing to get out of here, knowing that life in the old forms is not worth even one more moment of plugging along. Both extremes are there, both are real; both hold major keys to the Gemini soul.

As the bright cosmic future claims her, Gemini flips into a massively altered state of consciousness. Best of all, for the first time ever, something is asked of her that is entirely real and true. She is called upon to see and know and feel and act upon what is not possible in the old order, to fertilize the world from her inward sourcespring of perpetual renewal. At last this is something she can do with her whole multiple being.

Scorpio In Breath

Scorpio's persona is charged with a power both subtle and obvious. Fused with the utmost intensity of purpose and drive, all her acts bear grace and refinement. It is a combination that both draws and repels. What is hardest to resist about Scorpio is her central knowledgeability, her wisdom and certainty and piercing gaze. What pushes so many away is her superior air, her isolate style. She is very cold and deeply warm, and in her outer aspect the cold registers sharply and keeps the curious away.

Deeper in, the real story of Scorpio begins to unfold. She contains complete worlds, each one of which would be enough for anybody else. She is circulating freely amongst them and wielding all of them into sources of power, of truth, of deep feeling, of inward touch with what is most vital and essential. Her hidden worlds are not at all hidden to her. They are the heart of the real, the only thing that counts. Scorpio lives for the innermost layers and senses everything else from in there.

When on her own, Scorpio fashions and forges herself to be perfectly who she truly is. Yet she is not as intent upon solitude as might be projected upon her. For Scorpio is already and always alone, in deep, working within profound dimensions. She seeks renewal from the deepest communion with others and taps the alone spaces insouciantly. This is more a refresher course in what she already knows, always has indwelled timelessly.

At peak power the future awakenings of our times pierce through Scorpio. A major corner of her soul has been mutating exponential futures into being always. Yet as the future itself becomes so many worlds opening at once, Scorpio finds that her ultimate gifts are no longer shunned. She is the one who knows all worlds dynamically as one. We urgently require her capacity to draw us all through our lost spaces into the moment when history dissolves and the real inner knowledge, the worked substance of us blazes through.

The First Life Stream

The First House

Through the First House we receive into ourselves a distilled essence of who we *most essentially* are. We are given free rein to be with ourselves this life's journey.

Some wisdom is instinctual. A certain grace is felt and followed. A trenchant sensibility keeps throwing off conditionings and programmings and finding a place to be here.

We go through many changes in the First House while nothing ever changes, while what is constant means the most. Somebody inside keeps bearing down, keeps going further, keeps insisting upon authenticity and simplicity.

We struggle a lot nowadays with our First House. Having lost the art of letting ourselves be, we have yet to come to the skill which finds us when we are able to love from a deep center. We are caught in between tradition and vision, constancies and renewals. Our soul must have her own personal, individual container and basic allegiance to internal rhythms.

Yet it takes quite an attunement, a sensitivity, a substantive commitment to be able to get very far with qualities which, in more stable times than these, would nourish us and never let us down.

We are called to reconstitute all of the world within ourselves, to reinvent guidelines, to sense what is true to form. We can get scattered, distracted, confused, divided; then our First House planets may be enlisted to caretake, to make everything workable for our more avid selves and domains of involvement.

What lives inside a First House planet is ancient-future awareness, along with caring and attentiveness.

When we come unto ourselves afresh after losing center and direction, we at last begin to fathom the gifts and treasures we bear in the First House.

Each and every First House planet knows how to love, not only how to give but how to receive. The planets are steadying agents, especially for navigating through tortuous contemporary landscapes.

To tap the strength and source of the First House is a rare and precious magic. One typical situation is to grab hold of one vital quality and squeeze out of it everything we can. But a person who is in touch and in tune with the First House slows down, opens up, and creates a life space for things that were previously taken for granted.

Body wisdom and basic good sense are right there in the First House. It is simply a matter of remembering them and rededicating ourselves to them. There's a pulse beat to our existence, a subtle accompanying sound track that ushers us into and through each and every situation we meet *if we are really there.*

First House planets yank on us to get there, to stay there. The First House is the heart's path, the internal heart's path. It is about being tuned in, rather than being tuned out. Each and every First House planet is corded directly into our central trunk of purpose and of vision for this lifetime. Unfortunately we have set protective forces about us to keep the bulk of our soul receptivity either on hold or within manageable doses.

Yet still, the soul calls, the heart urges. Something comes into our world, something we least expected, and suddenly everything looks so very different. The First House is our promise to ourselves, our vow to return, to remember, to stay true.

We wander as far from this place as we possibly can; all the while subconsciously we count on our rising sign and our First House planets to rein us in, to restore perspective and wholeness.

In these post-millennial times we now enter, a door has been flung open—so that our First House intimations and gleanings, hunches and hopes begin to find their pattern and to move through long-standing blocks and obstacles.

The feminine life force is at peak bouquet, flavor, and consistency in the First House; that essence permeates and restores and draws us through our being and beyond it. Inside the First House what we inherit from all ancient worlds will serve the future. Our own selves are the crossing point, the bridge; we are both/and.

We are called in the First House to listen, to watch, to notice, and to reap the dividends of constant attending to what counts. We are merged within our First House qualities, identified with them, attached to them, lost inside of them, and restored to ourselves through them. They are the sacred fount, often polluted and defiled, ever intact and resonant. The First House is where we are most intimately ourselves, most immune to distorting or denying our birthright. There *is* a Divine blueprint and we find ourselves carrying it through, hoping toward forever, just as always.

Taurus

Taurus is the one sign of the zodiac we have forgotten how to live and embody. The nature of Taurus is to take hold of favorable components in the life surroundings in order to align oneself with what is natural and simple, what is here and shared amongst us.

Taurus wants badly to please, to help, to fill a need, to be of substantive worth. Taurus craves approval and recognition, ongoing and steady acknowledgment. Taureans so often fail to live their own lives' solitude, to be here with their own true journey.

Called upon over and again to recover the spark, to realize the soul gifts inside, Taurus tends to be shadowed by collective anguish. In modern times this can be disabling. Just by tapping inherent attributes, Taurus can forge a clear, strong new way forward.

Given what self-abandonment and self-neglect can do to us, it is very hard for Taurus to carry her own instinctual journey wakefully and stay right with it. For example, Taurus greatly delights in being rhythmically useful on a daily basis—an abusable quality in self-intoxicated times.

Many Taureans develop a thick skin, a stuck-unto-themselves quality. The disturbances they suffer are a form of selfhood that seeks an intimate and sustaining context. In effect, Taurus is hyper-susceptible to the undercurrent of our times, so forced to dig deeper and explore further in order to make any headway.

The traditional sign of basic life maintenance needs to cultivate a different way to live.

The first stage of recovery involves after losing the self in everything but self, regaining a measure of perspective. But for this to bear fruit, Taurus needs to move out beyond the private self-contained clusters of the past. Then a tremendous discovery begins to unfold. It can come from the outside or the inside; it can come slowly or very fast. Taurus gets wind of a different kind of breeze—that one's own internal nature is a source point, a vital springboard, is, in fact, the one who has kept the home fires burning and not forgotten the heart's call.

Once Taurus does value the self and honor its instincts and impulses, a very different story is enacted, almost unrecognizable in our present context. The one who was less than self flows forth in a fullness that even opens doors for others.

It is simply a matter of tending the garden in this dimension faithfully. The character traits and essence qualities that Taurus cultivates— a missing ingredient from our times— will be as strong, clear, and helpful as they are truly personalized. Taurus must form a basis for selfhood in communion with the good graces all around her.

If Taurus tunes deeper and taps the inner well creatively, she encounters a depth of reference, a range of feeling tone previously left almost unknown. It is as though a medicinal weed that was always growing right here is suddenly called for.

If you spring Taurus from all the tune-out contexts, she becomes the one who stays right in here with everybody, understanding perfectly. She is the soul of this planet, the keeper of the flame of common things.

The essence of Taurus sparks new worlds into being. What a journey it takes to honor these things, to encounter them more deeply!

Taurus lives in the Earth in the salt-of-the-earth soul; she elicits what is here in the roots amongst us.

Brilliant when sufficiently quickened, dull when left to the side, Taurus is the seeds, the roots, the grass, the topsoil, the component that fertilizes and restores equanimity. Almost everything about Taurus is happening on the inner belt, in worlds apart.

For those of us who are alive in our imagination and rediscovering how to live in this planet authentically, the Taurean dimension becomes our first lesson in what we are summoned to, likewise the warning to how we can miss this call so easily. Taurus is about fostering, acknowledging self unto self, world unto self, self unto world. Miss the first step, and all that follows is off-kilter. Step into a fake Earth at the Taurean stage, and all future life streams will be mere metaphors and fantasies.

Pushing her way further to the inside in order to call forth the life forces of those here for this planet and her changes, Taurus bears the goddess intact within and deposits her treasure where alone it can bring a New Earth into being. Her most intimate fiber is instilled with what endures, and she must express that through as her life deed.

Venus

Venus gets through to us. Her style is to feed us what we need and what we desire, yet simultaneously to deprive us of the super fullness we try to dream up for ourselves.

Venus is feminine wise. No one can come forward further until he has what he wants and needs and then discovers something much deeper is lacking, is calling, is still untapped. The fast majority cannot come forward yet.

Venus has an amazing ability to lead us through the maze of the world's ways. She hosts. She welcomes. She offers the guided tour. Each one of us is surprised and startled when what we hoped and dreamed is shattered. Each one of us is given our real chance only once our hopes and dreams are shattered.

Venus is the innate, internally driven feeling for the whole territory of life. She is the quality check, the one who determines how we really feel after all.

Venus is as free, as alive, as life-giving as we let her be. Her way is to pull us further through, to guide us, between the lines, to ask for more, dream further, seek something beyond comfort and security.

Venus is the intact inner voice of a knowingness and beingness that absolutely will see us through. She never loses her internal treasure, for she secretly replenishes herself from the universal source spring.

We all believe in Venus but have a hard time staying true to her. She is compelling, bracing, unimpressed by considerations and external trappings. She cuts to the quick.

Often in our culture, Venus has hidden herself, has been intentionally deceptive, because we don't honor this goddess in a living way. She will not tolerate such treatment. She will find her ways to suffuse the landscape with feeling, with whatever part of soul we have forgotten and cast into shadow.

Venus must bring to our attention how we really feel inside. Forceful and persistent, she is good at bringing us back to ourselves when we have become surface fixated and outwardly driven. She is constantly practicing how to restore wholeness, to bring people together, to reconcile them, to heal. She insists that we *can* come together, for she remembers how it's meant to be.

For many of us, Venus operates primarily as our soul's accompaniment, our intimate internal companion. When we do love, Venus comes into her own. She has a far more extravagant impulse to share when there is passion, creative engagement with life as a whole. Then Venus clicks into deep resonance. Linking us back with whatever and whomever is most vital to us, she compels us to be on fire with each day's promises.

Venus has a tremendous bias, a very strong leaning. She seeks and identifies with whatever fans the flames of life, of love. Generously and inclusively she delights in and makes the most of all versions of camaraderie, of rapport, of chemistry.

Being there with the life flow in wonder and amazement, Venus is ultimately untamable. She slips right out of all the places in which we try to capture her. In truth, we cannot even hold an image, a steady picture of Venus, before she shape-changes into something quite different.

Venus makes each being summon something to meet what others are retrieving from within themselves. Venus gets it; she catches the way it really goes. She is just subtle enough, multidimensional enough to stay tuned, deep and far enough to accompany us wherever we need to go.

Venus is a smile, a bursting joy, a sudden flowering. She is what the feminine becomes when stripped of distorting reflections. Venus is the stillpoint awaiting our quieting down and once again tuning to subtler frequencies.

More than anything she ever does, Venus serves to make the sacred ordinary, to make the ordinary sacred. It is the absolute Venusian sensibility that the common and extraordinary, the exquisite and ordinary are sisters delighting in each other's company. Venus must include; she must find a yes.

Those of us who serve her faithfully are greatly blessed to find that there are bottomless rooms inside of Venus to explore and discover. We give things away and find them everywhere once again. Venus is the taproot, the wonder worker, so she cannot bear to deny the life spark where it arises; we would do well to honor and appreciate her beneficent presence in our midst.

The Second Life Stream

The Second House

We arrive upon the shores of the Second House with a special longing, something pressing to come through us. If we respond, we will find that all the world around us belongs to us and that we are a snug fit. We are being ushered into the regions of our deeper self with its many claims. Once, we left our best in this region to be picked up later, and now it is time to make good on our promises.

An acute instinct for truth and for reality drives us to stay present within ourselves, to be here for this journey of the soul through the world. We must stay on a line of central conviction, of deepest destiny. In this house we will be tested, sorely tested, perhaps more than in any other.

Future forces are available to speed us as far and fast as we need. But there is one thorny requirement. We must over and again give ourselves over, truly recognize that it is a greater self we serve and only that way can we achieve true value.

Do we have the interior resiliency to withstand stark evidence to the contrary? What will we do when it seems that we are thwarted, held back, grossly denied, and negated? Where will we go when we are not understood and seen? What will be our inner voice's response or reaction when there is no outer proof that we are supported and encouraged by the whole of existence to come to ourselves?

In the Second House each one of us is submitted to this trial repeatedly. In cadent breaks the truth shines through, providing openings at which we not only see and feel but know that what we bear is welcome and needed. However, if we get inflated by exploiting such cycles, we will find ourselves back in the testing grounds, shown once again that we have yet to entrust ourselves to the Living Spirit and its enigmatic ways.

The Second House is a rare place, in that only treasures are able to stay here. All false values and pragmatic ideas soon prove fallow. We are asked to strip down to only essential items of value in recognition we can no longer get away with an externalized mental operating style. It is as though all of existence were waiting upon us. What will we decide? Which way will we go?

Certainly during the twentieth century, the Second House was included among the common and ordinary things, hardly given a second thought. We actually forgot that we bear with us from before great plenitude, inward understandings, depths of soul experience. When we lost the track of positive karmas on an individual level, we began to believe that we were captured by phenomena themselves, trapped in this world, lost in time. Societal factors seemed to confirm this assessment. We gave up on our real selves and played the game of: what could we think up in its place that might do just as well?

Then we proceeded to live our lives by a mentally-contrived shell self, keeping the real cache-bearer in an attic we barely knew was there. Typically it took extreme crises, life-shattering ordeals to draw forth from within us she-who-always-awaits.

In the twentieth century our core destiny was held away from us. We collaborated with extant forces to set things up this way. Superficially it felt like a relief—because to express in this world our innate treasures would inevitably expose us to the fate of differentness, isolation, and ostracism. Throughout the course of the century we lost heart for that battle. Too many atrocities. Too leaden a weight to bear.

We are called to emerge through the Second House and the planets we place therein. We are asked to access once again what we still bear within us intact. Our gifts and assets are patient and faithful. They expectantly await our change of heart.

Each one's Second House is the most prodigious repository of value, of resource, of goods that we inherit from our own past life selves. This is where we grant ourselves absolutely anything we need. Nobody can ever exhaust or deplete the reservoir of their Second House planets.

Often in self-defense, these planets become prickly and mental. They guard their turf; they stare suspiciously at strangers. There is much good *in here,* but it is hard to bring it forth because there has been such rampant corruption *out there.* We sometimes turn in on ourselves in reaction, trying to hoard what we were given in cosmic generosity, to hang onto it, make it pay.

Truly everything here is meant to pass through us. Our Second House planets are ultimately just watching over sacred vestiges and keeping them whole. No matter what else we do, propagation is essential, for we are here to give the world life.

Virgo

The sign Virgo is so very blessed, so very cursed, so very gifted, so very easily misled. The blessings and the bounties abound to such an extent that there is no sign more favored by the Goddess Natura, by the forces of Earth. She is indeed the darling of this world. Virgo bears everything within her that this world thirsts and hungers for.

Virgo's most exquisite asset lies in the way she beholds and witnesses the gifts and virtues of others. She is entirely capable of granting each one she loves a new start, a departure into a radically revitalized cycle. And in one way or another, this is her intent throughout her life. She is called to manifest in the flesh, to draw forth, to allow and make room for whatever each one bears. This is also her own salvation—to be able to work in this way, to serve so rightfully.

It is even possible, in the rare case of one who has matured and ripened past twentieth-century standards, for Virgo to partake in the actual wonders occurring. This is what she asks and what she needs. Her great call is for someone to do for her what she does for others. Perhaps it will be her own self that ultimately responds to that call.

If Virgo is unfertilized by the feeling of self-completeness, if she hasn't yet met that rare destiny of being there within herself as she is within others, she must then seek on the outside. And Virgo most often does seek endlessly on the outside. She seeks there, while also withholding herself, as if she knew she wouldn't find what she looked for. And so there is a motif in Virgo of that which reaches out, yet (at the same time) does not freely and truly reach out. Sadly, if we come to the surface and manifest there with a half-hearted gesture of wanting and needing, yet not trusting and believing, this reaps a harvest of suffering and prolonged ordeals.

In the thick of the pain and the struggle, Virgo is activating an in-between state, a neither-here-nor-there place. This is excruciating for her, yet necessary and inevitable. She has made a reality-assessment that is not only questionable but has terrible consequences for her. In conceding what was not likely to come her way, in presuming that the world is as it is and you cannot change it, Virgo has betrayed herself. She has imposed an arbitrary limit, a ceiling and a floor, close walls, a tight chamber to live in. But it is her mind that is the jailer and the enforcer.

Each hard inch of this plight can be reversed. Virgo must tap her reserve goddess powers, those forbidden fruits, to call in her helpers, to mobilize the spirit brigade, to get something moving here. She cannot passively submit to what she has wrought. The entire pivot of her life's journey turns upon being willing and able to ask, to call, to know that she is authorized to receive and to move with a mediating force, to shift her own perspective and reality.

It is Virgo's destiny to return from the dead, to restore what was lost, to become what she seemed fated to miss and lose and deny. It is her capacity, like no other sign, to come again from another place, to annex what she was blinded to.

In order to make this possible, she must over and again learn the super-fine art of letting go. That involves not just being easy-going or carefree, but rather letting her whole spirit lead her in a movement, a releasing breath. She must become able to imagine in the moment that all those burdens are transient and are no longer needed, and that she will remain strong and clear, once these are removed from her life space.

Virgo has one consistent challenge to confront in life. She sees the world as huge, herself as less formidable. It is this distortion which lays her low. Therefore, her path is to discover her vastness within and then to find that there is room for this vastness in every world she enters.

The self-structure of Virgo is complex and multifaceted. She is both egoistic and self-denying, both astute and seduced by the trappings of the outer mind. It is her very nature to be many things in one—many voices, myriad angles of approach. Once she understands herself, she does not need to be singular or consistent. And the task of understanding herself stands before her every day, imbedded in the fine details of every situation she meets.

The beauty of Virgo is that she knows the Earth and the Earth knows her. Almost everything that lets her be is of the Earth. And Virgo shines forth with the timeless splendor of this Earth's mysteries and secrets and hidden depths everywhere.

Most extraordinary about Virgo is that, if you peel away layers, there are always more. For Virgo has wrapped herself around her own inner self several times, and it takes a series of initiatory breakthroughs to crack the code. Virgo is entrusted with a memory, a soul-faculty sacred and magical. In her cells, in her very being, Virgo recalls what has been, what is source wisdom. She regains what is most vital in what we think of as the past, but it is really that other room right next door. It is just as much the future.

Virgo is the summation of history, the bearer of the generations, the Daughter of Gods and Goddesses and worlds beyond telling. She is here for a short while, gracing us by her presence. What she must find in her brief moment is a giving and a receiving, a love that is sufficiently true to reach inside her private soul. Without that, Virgo pines away.

Virgo craves solitude, but not too much of it. With love and under-standing, she is warmed and transformed. For she is the mystery gath-erer, the great seeker and finder of what this life is all about.

Vesta

We have misused the asteroids in the nineteenth and twenti-eth centuries. During the nineteenth, what we did with those heavenly bodies was to propagandize ourselves into cities, mass consciousness, and the near-obliteration of the personal soul. During the twentieth, we intensified this current to the max, adding a planetary grid to pen us in.

We have treated the asteroids as our hiding places from ourselves, from our greater truth, and from our mission in this planet.

The twenty-first century is destined to be the one in which we learn how to tap the asteroids regeneratively. Yet the end of the twentieth century, just before this point of freeing up, has featured an extreme barrage of negative asteroidal control mechanisms, as though to fore-stall the inevitable breakthroughs.

We must view any given of the four major asteroids within the framework of both the ravages we have endured in its name and the entirely divergent direction in which each asteroid can take us from this point on.

The dated version of Vesta is devoted to shifting our traditional per-spective on ordinary existence from a more wholesome and affirma-tive approach through the anxiety-ridden and frustration-focused sense of outer everyday practicalities of late. Vesta accompanies us on this passage, actually guiding us into the worst of it, and then beyond. But in our subjective experience, Vesta registers as virtually a blanket reinforcement to our most fundamental dreads and avoidances. Vesta says that basic outer existence is one big headache, while she simul-taneously draws us into it and out of it.

Her underlying strategy is to make us face the dark side of our minds. She is convinced that only when we have exhausted completely our critical mind faculties, our negative feedback loops, will we be able to carry forward from here with some measure of self-support and sense of sanctuary inside a live world.

This is a devastatingly effective approach. We live out our most banal nightmare of overt existence *having no place for us, yet demanding that we comply with it and its laws.* And that's called life. And that's called "you only live once, so go for it." And we can talk ourselves into the proposition that this will go on forever and that somehow it doesn't really matter anyway because not only will it go on forever but it—we—will disappear, to it, to ourselves, and to everyone else. We become false stoics, helplessly resigned to what we conceive to be a sociocultural fate—all because we're in that kind of world and don't know our way out again.

The finishing touch to this so-very-common predicament is that Vesta then often will push herself into obligations and cycles where she seems locked and devoid of real ways through. She fixes things so that every factor conspires to make us stay in there until we get the point of what it is like to be at the mercy of a false world with no true buffers to keep us alive and clear.

The entire picture of Vesta-in-action applies to the nineteenth and twentieth centuries. Her change at hand now is immense. As with the other asteroids, she will necessarily unfold in steps and stages. And the first steps will seem to be modest and unthreatening to the structures of the old.

Her basic initial probe out beyond the world net of the mass-control society tells her that she needs to heal herself, to get back in touch with who she is as a living being. Typically, a tiny movement in this direction will turn out to be very big indeed. For as Vesta sets herself the task of healing and returning, so many forms must be uprooted. The many selves she left behind are there thronging, offering suggestions, urgent to come forth again and be part of life.

Vesta brings with her a hard-won appreciation for how common things are woven from Nature's loom and need to be sustained from within. They are not merely mechanically functional and conducted from the outer mind's habitual grooves. As she grows into this dawning realization of the organic and the wondrous harvest that is life in this Earth, Vesta metamorphoses into a wildly different place.

It is Vesta's destiny as a regenerative twice-born living being to uncover subtle factors, to serve intricate mysteries, to restore common life. She becomes a witness of and participant in everyday miracles, none of which were regular and normal before. Her existence takes off into what she always knew it was meant to be. And the best part is that she is right there—sober, accounted for, precisely present in each magical pristine moment.

Vesta has learned that her inner instincts were right all along. Just before she took on the social program, she knew what she then forgot. And as she restores these knowings, something of the deepest significance shifts.

It was Vesta's tendency to take her reality for granted. This familiar residue had always been there, a part of her. So she had to give over, had to seem to lose identity before she could honor it.

Those who hold the key to common ordinary existence, to living in this planet rhythmically, are greatly blessed, but only insofar as they open to their secret heart. Exile is indeed the fate of Vesta until it is time to come home to Earth, to body, to the hearth flames burning away in the center of the world —never gone, brighter than ever.

Jupiter

Jupiter's vision floods in our veins. It is in every cell. It leaps forth in all directions at once. Jupiter is multi-dimensional, future potent. And her power is centered in our brow, in our true mind, in the part of us which leads us from obscurity to the truth beyond memory.

Jupiter shines brightest in those of us who have the capacity for collective evolution. She wants to be engaged within the whole of existence—the bigger and more demanding, the better. For she is vast and she is limitless and she commands respect and adherence.

The interior challenge along the Jupiter pathway is to wake up. She wishes us to gain awareness between the lines, amongst the spaces, and not so much straight on. Jupiter is skillful and adroit, wise to the way the outer mind operates. She knows better than anybody how to outwit attempts by outer mind to hang onto the status quo, to insist on security against her own mighty blows.

It is Jupiter's way to sneak up on us, to weave a spell, to fashion a garment, to surround us and envelop us; yet when we look for her she is gone. She has an axial job to do. Everything rides on the successful fulfillment of her task. It is top priority, absolutely.

She must bring us to ourselves despite ourselves. She must make us see ourselves, even though we are allergic to such a sight. She must restore our memory and (while we sleep in so many other respects) renew our vision inward. It is Jupiter's job to impart that we are perfect and deserving. She is the goddess of tough and impossible projects. She is one who is always called in to redeem and transmute, alchemically, to do a whole incredible number on our fatally flawed and miserably unwilling selves.

Jupiter delights in our absurd predicaments. She rolls up her sleeves when we are finished and done for. This one-planet relief-crew supplies us with our most desperately needed component—hope. She infuses us with the most unreasonable and irrepressible kind of hope and confidence and sense of well-being, arising in the most unlikely places and times and never quitting.

Jupiter is tailor-made for our dire predicaments. What she does is to bring us into the future, there to restore all perspective and greater faculties. Then in a flash we are back, right where we were. But something has changed. We are willing, where we were previously fading out.

The whole stream of Jupiter has been renewing itself radically in the late twentieth century. A huge comet shattered the old Jupiter in 1994 and made her scramble to come to us in a whole new form. That recongealment is the intervener, the mediator, the orchestrator/spirit-on-the-spot. Jupiter has been shifted from her aloof perch of old to a full-on participation in the grittiest marl.

She has even switched from masculine to feminine. Her revolutionary message is to tap our intelligence to heal and transform this planet in small ways as well as big ones. She is shifting our rational focus from degenerative and divisive and decadent stuff to responsive alacrity, seeking whole new ways to see and know and be. Protean, multiple, Jupiter has become the spirit of the age. What we need from her now is a spark, a boost for a human species that is worn out from too many battles with itself that it keeps losing.

Jupiter is showing up on our common horizon. And she brings all the planets beyond her with her. She and all the rest were previously blackballed by the asteroids. Anything that stretched us too far was condemned by the asteroids as excessive, useless. So it took a big explosion to get the cosmos back in focus.

Sculpting out an intimate space for each one of us to imagine again is the Jovian impulse of our times. When we find ourselves suddenly able to conceive what we previously shut out, Jupiter is at work. But there is one side to Jupiter that we still cannot handle, a side that hangs over the near future, waiting for us to become grounded and centered enough to absorb the shock of the ultimate Jupiterian dimension of inspiration.

That cosmic side of Jupiter, still undigested collectively, concentrates upon celebrating our human nature as divine. It acknowledges that we are here as bridge to an exceedingly unlikely greater future. Our pragmatic minds fervently resist this scope and magnitude. For we don't want to be fooled and disappointed again.

Yet, the cosmic Jupiter keeps on coming. It portends a way of life in which living beings in this planet illuminate from within and can no longer resist our own birthright. A tone of pervasive celebration, rolling and carefree, accompanies cosmic Jupiter.

The occasions of Jupiter that do show up amongst us—despite what we believe or don't believe, or almost believe because of these self-same tendencies—tend to cluster around the very thing we most would not let ourselves picture as being possible. Suddenly it is showing up as where our actual destiny goes. We are "blown away." Somebody in us revives miraculously; somebody in us dies away.

Jupiter is the hostess, the choreographer of the world transformations of the twenty-first century. She knows how to give us a very good time, a high time. What she has in store, nobody knows. She is adept at not letting us have our rigid prophesies, at not letting our dooms and glooms come out the way we insist on hatching and conceiving them. For somebody else is in charge here. And she is so spunky and so hard to refuse that all of us will get it and bow before the feminine Jupiter, the one who knows what we can't yet and starts from there.

The Third Life Stream

The Third House

We never really show up in the Third House. Instead, we send in the clowns. We meet the surface life in ways which cut us off from ourselves; we gather mere stock fragments. This generates a lot of space and many chances. We can do almost anything, become each moment's magical possibilities. But something is missing here. The gap we sense—if we are willing to go there—is our one real opening. And it takes a lot of guts to come back alive.

The way the story goes: we were vibrantly in tune with how everything really felt until we hit adolescence. Then we spun out to be part of the fun, to join the festivities. There were far too many of them. And we kept going further out, until our life connection snapped. We were split between surface and depth. And whatever we did out on the surface couldn't any longer reach through to where we were inside. We entered a peer-sibling world, and we have been in it ever since. Making adjustments, concessions, we enjoy life from the outside in.

But many of us are blessed to feel the surge of the planetary awakening, right here in the Third House. This comes on subliminally as a more urgent and critical force field. It gradually overrides the conditioned circuits of getting along with the crowd. The planetary awakening becomes synchronized with our bodily wisdom, drawing us forth vitally. Deeper instincts tapped, our previous mass-societal identification starts to feel remote and old.

We are blessed to live in extraordinary times. Our Third House planets tip over into a different model, another style. But—because we have developed this tenacious habit of hiding out, of camouflaging our aliveness and reality in socially acceptable forms—we have a lot to learn, a lot of ground to make up. As we enter the stripping zone (albeit with lots of resistance), we stall as long as we can before we begin to expose ourselves to direct experience, naked.

If it were not for the Earth needing us to come out from under, we probably never would. In a personal sense, it has been so convenient to live our outer lives on automatic, to live secret lives in a safe isolate corner. But now the convergence is at hand; we have to close the gap.

We knew this call would come; our visceral instincts alerted us ahead of time. So many of us have made sure to keep the collective trance light and permeable. Whatever strategy we took on, whenever we took it on, the time is now at hand; the energy wave of the future is everywhere you look. And in this body there is a resonance, a relief, a sense of almost being flooded by memories, each showing the element we have lost track of.

Our Third House planets are fundamentally desperate to free themselves from shallow frequencies and from places we choose to go for all the wrong reasons. Indeed, the return journey from escapism, addictions and so many hiding places is an extended, serpentine, shamanic passage. We will need to gather our wits about us and start paying much closer attention to what is close at hand—the signs, the synchronicities are snowballing. We need to fine-tune our knack, the skill of being in the right place at the right time, to make a world (literally) of difference.

There is a map, a method and a way to do this. First, you orient toward needing to go deeper, moving from distraction and stimulus orientation to being present within this body in this living moment. Then you fashion the vessel, most of which involves becoming proprioceptively aware, sense attuned, giving up anything that impedes the free flow of life force. All of this is to get ready, to be sharper and clearer.

The planetary changes will ask us to activate our life passion in a way that reclaims the Earth and our bodies within the Earth. Inside the Third House we can easily get swept away by certain groups and streams which promise marvelous things, yet deliver us into bondage.

To cut through this trap, we must recite again and again that the future belongs to everybody and that only a truly universal, inclusive, and charitable, loving approach can serve. When we have so little margin for error, we need to cut away at the luxuriant undergrowth of self-serving notions and flattering, gratifying ways out.

The path with heart that is truly collective will be arduous. Yet it will keep drawing us deeper, and it likely will not make us seem super-special in the old style. The live spirit within this Earth craves and needs our quickening pulse of honest, steady presence. If we can get there for the planet, we will fulfill our capacity in just the way it was meant to be forged, as close accompaniment to all sentient beings everywhere coming into freedom together.

Sagittarius

If our own rhythms and live energy forces match and mesh within what is happening in the world around us, we are inside of Sagittarius, and we are going to have quite a journey to move through it. We are naturally from birth in sympathetic resonance with our immediate surroundings and with what others want and need us to do and be. We respond instinctively and almost instantaneously to that energy wave and its shared consciousness over the course of our lives. If we could, we would make everybody happy and share freely of ourselves spontaneously and effortlessly. We have everything to offer, and our world gives open arms to what we bear.

However, even though in Sagittarius we will try to convince ourselves and everybody else over and again that this situation is optimal and delightful—this meshing of self and world—it is in fact a lot of trouble. One of the pivotal dilemmas we can never get away from is that a real living self has many layers of awareness, of expression, and of participation. Most life contexts reward and amplify our outermost layers of personality, while having little place for more substantive soul layers. The consequence is that we can have a great time acting out worldly and clever, sophisticated and charming facets of self without sufficiently growing and evolving to support and give depth to our actual display of those very qualities. This pattern tends to thin out, burn out, lose its edge, and deteriorate into cycles of frustration, disillusionment, and profound despondency. We are compelled in Sagittarius to teach ourselves how to renew, to revitalize, to restore our native stock of life force and primal awareness.

Until we become adept in the subtle life arts, our Sagittarian syndrome is to adopt a sequence of roles and easy identities, for the sake of outer considerations of every kind, while bailing out of the real deeper path we are meant to walk. The self-willed sticking to these less-than-fulfilling ways of life (for all the best reasons) apparently is the fatal flaw in the Sagittarian character. Getting away with absence and tune-out is the great Sagittarius fantasy. Sooner or later a hunger for something more than this comes into play. Then the real fun begins.

The all-time favorite Sagittarius occupation or activity is to learn something new, to practice and train and develop fresh skills. The later stages of the Sagittarian life-path key on this quality. Sagittarius is sparked by the challenge of destiny to overthrow a false self who has been put in charge up to this point. We need to become aware of ourselves in a reliable way, to be willing day after day to overcome pride and intellect by facing (without any further rationalizations and justifications) where we are now, what is motivating us, why we really are here.

In mature Sagittarian passage, we want to know the truth and we don't care if it hurts. What this leads into inevitably is an evolving beyond personal separative absorptions into a remembering of the wider circle to which we belong. Sagittarius does a miserable job of gratifying and fulfilling narcissistic desires and needs. We can sate them forever and never get anywhere.

Any true act of giving ourselves to life must be authentic to be evolutionarily on the beam. We have no choice but to work out our own gargantuan appetite for self-reinforcement, for being everybody's most familiar figure. Along Sagittarius frequencies, experience is what counts; making endless mistakes is the most likely way through.

Ultimately, there is a mastery inside of Sagittarius. The final hurdle to releasing that gift is the need to be right, the need to be wrong, the need to play out rights and wrongs endlessly. The wiser one inside is neither pragmatic nor idealistic, neither righteously virtuous nor chaotically implosive. In the center deep down in, Sagittarius is pulling for a world beyond dualities and polarizations. To draw the self all the way down in there demands an endless process, without any further protests and complaints, of surrendering, letting go, admitting and acknowledging fundamental realities.

The sign of Sagittarius is an exceedingly difficult one to awaken within. There are so many trances, so many dormancies. Few stay with it long enough. But then again, what this zodiac sign most essentially is about is living out illusions until they burst open.

We are collectively lost inside of Sagittarius, adrift in its vapors. Visionaries and pioneers are needed to pierce the disguise and salvage the gist of a sign absolutely loaded with talent and smarts. Those who take on the Sagittarian inner quest receive tremendous encouragement and guidance from the forces of evolution. Nonetheless, it would take a furious depth of commitment to leap through the Sagittarius shadow. This is the energy which confounds us at every turn, the energy which infuses us with courage to battle through our own insidious traps and vast bramble-fields (as thick and deep as World War II was in the middle of the century). It is the energy and courage to forge on and never say die. Sagittarius is the sign we all love, we all despair of, and we all root for, avidly and with incorrigible conviction that the impossible will happen this time around.

Neptune

What we all have most in common is Neptune. It is the subtext, the underlying story. If we are conscious of Neptune, she is not doing a very good job of working her magic. Her entire stream deepens upon subterfuge, trickery, slipping in and out. Neptune is taking us through an initiation of a major scope, of staggering magnitude.

Her way with us is to inundate our subtle senses with enough powerful psychic energy to make us lose track of her in a dreamy, suggestible, passive receptivity. Then Neptune draws our deep inner soul, in alignment with the collective soul, into and through the planetary initiation of the will. This involves reversing the flow of self-will to become a vehicle for a greater will. The personal egoic drive will never sit still for such lessons and shifts. Therefore, it must be knocked out to make room—a delicate process.

On inner planes, Neptune is a charged, dynamic, full-blooded presence. Her task is to carve out a space for the sacred to pour through. Under optimal conditions, Neptune will empty us of our busy mind, our roller- coaster emotions, and will place us firmly inside of a frequency and energy wave. It is perhaps full of mystery and magic, yet quintessentially simple and straightforward. Exposure to this optimal Neptune spirals us to the inside and makes it self-evident that all the deeper inner worlds and influences are more here than ever and can bring us through if we first yield control and then build up a co-creative sensibility.

Our innermost soul awaits us at the heart of Neptune. Yet to claim her, we must be driven right out of our stronghold of personal positioning. Neptune takes everything away, all our props. But, correspondingly, she restores the inward version of everything we give over. When we take Neptune up on her challenge to us, we start to be a soul inside a continuum.

There is however one great test and trial that Neptune often insists upon. For a time we cannot stay with ourselves in a convincing fashion; instead we feel self-abandoned. Deep underneath this place we relive past lifetimes, every kind of agonizing memory fragment. Subjectively we are drowning in multiple pasts, unconnected energetically to any present stabilizing time. There arise panic and terror, pervasive anxiety and free-floating meaninglessness—loss of direction altogether. A whirlpool sucks us down. When this homeless state comes upon us, we are at the center of the shadow side of the Neptune initiation—a cold, cyclonic planet, large and faraway from the nucleus, the hearth.

Navigating through this soul condition is the hardest thing we will ever do. Our forces are fragmented, atomized, scattered. We feel no center, no core to orient around. Those who survive this ordeal have consistently found that their first step has to be against their survival instinct, saying yes to this experience, not denying it. The turbulent waters begin to calm when we realize somehow that we are not making this up, that it is really happening this way, and that it needs to be taken all the way through (even if it seems crazy or impossible). The deep message coming through the shadow Neptune initiation is that we cannot cling to the self we used to be (in what seemed like forever) and that a more viable and true-to-Spirit self is on its way, if we can be there for ourselves in this ozone passage from one world to another.

Neptune is intent upon turning us inside-out and upside-down. All of this is to counter the corruptions and the distortions, the socialized self husk which stands in our way. The Neptunian voyage makes total sense from the deep center, yet so often (from any outward point of view) seems surpassingly strange. Rarely is it clear where the curve came from, why the bottom dropped out.

To spiritual beings who are involved with the Neptunian process, the inexplicable curves are simply crafty ways to do magic, are where magic is outlawed.

Rationalistically, Neptune is absurd. Only as we become tuned into the mystic core of life does the chaos of Neptune prove to be orderly, systematic, tremendously coherent, and effective.

In the final reckoning, Neptune is a collective planet, taking all of us through wild passages from one world to another. The orchestrators of this find their way through Neptune beautifully. They elude all our attempts to label and outwit them. Spirit forces are fully in charge here. When we become actively co-creative with them, evolution quantum-leaps forward. In the Neptune dispensation, what baffles us outwardly is bringing us homeward inwardly. We will get it when we are ready. Our own true self rides the Neptune waves with abandon crying, "Join me, the dance is about to begin."

The Fourth Life Stream

The Fourth House

We are located inside the Earth Root, within the deep body, the deep soul. We are under, living from under. Outer mind forbids us to navigate consciously in this fashion. So we stay hidden and seek to manifest our dreams within the surface world as the only thing that matters.

To be dwelling on a regular basis in spaces that have so little outer currency and such a great inner charge is sobering and humbling. We are delegated the lesson of accepting and embracing, of surrendering to the outer fate of seeming to be lost under somewhere. Even more, we are slowly introduced to the crying need to acknowledge internally where we really are and what we are doing inside the Undersoul, where nobody is supposed to be.

That we are actually tapping a deep Earth source keeps us going. We get into the Fourth House through our family of origin, our first home, our initial community experience in this lifetime. Most of us experience there that while we are met on the outside, we are refused on the inside. This dichotomy initially splits us between the one who adapts and the one who stays under. When this becomes our way of life, this split, we unconsciously reach to our deep Earth source to keep the hidden one going. The surface one may act out an innocuous existence as programmed by the ancestors, but the deep one is sent far under. There he finds he belongs to the Living Earth.

Because the adaptive personality in the Fourth House is so shallow and predictable, we shall not track that layer here, other than to say that there may be appearances over an extended cycle deceiving us there is nothing much happening in the Fourth House. Our planets here may look dormant, latent. Nonetheless, let us take the journey of the deep soul in the deep body. Let us see what is truly going on underneath. Let us excavate the value and meaning of Fourth House planets.

The one who lives under is dreaming, is wishing, is awash in deep emotions; he feels lost, held. It is, for a while, a suspended existence. But there is something else going on, further in. Each Fourth House planet is being molded, sculpted, carved out. It is being prepared for what shall be. It is held inside a creative process that is critical. This is its reason for being.

The creative process is actually a healing and a restoring of lost faculties, of ancient memories, of future capacities. It is a timeless frequency of giving the soul back to herself when she is most lost, furthest in exile. It happens globally and personally—each being fed into this hopper. It is where all futures shall arise. The womb of the New Earth is here.

We become secretly a part of what shall be, what once was, what always is. Because of this secret source-spring, our Fourth House planets are on tap for resource-requiring situations, where no other planet can handle what is called for. Our Fourth House planets come from a wisdom that sustains life.

However, we do also endure our greatest tragedies and heartaches in this house. This is where we cannot go on, where we feel depressed or despondent, entirely victimized or fatally self-thwarting. It is very hard to get a handle on who we are here, where we are going. Everything is so elusive and insubstantial. Therefore, we outwardly suffer and die many deaths inside the Fourth House. Most of us know this part better than any other.

How can we move from a conditioned sense of being doomed and forsaken into the taproot sense of being an integral link in Earth existence? The answer is: we have to go deeper *despite ourselves*. We have to take seriously the emotions and physical symptoms of our loss. The call here is to sink inside, instead of holding on just above what we are feeling. If we can assimilate what is really in there, then this New

Creation that is stirring inside us will reach through and connect to us. This is natural. It is inevitable. Of course, we resist it massively.

To plunge deeper and keep feeling, to identify within what is officially not even there, to have the courage to be with ourselves in the depths are the keys to fulfilling the Fourth House. Our fears are so wild and rampant—our anxieties even more so. Yet we have come down this far in order to remember and realize. What is it we left behind? Where did we go?

Being truly inside the Fourth House—the Earth Root— is a matter of honoring our root self, regardless of what any outer mind tells us is happening. In the thick of our skepticisms, we must begin the new world within ourselves by saying yes to the root self in all its pain and struggle. We must be self-compassionate, even after developing the worldly habit of self-abandonment and self-betrayal.

The truth of who we are underneath wants to be known, wants to be lived, wants to be taken as the basis for a more authentic future. Yet it requires many wrenchings to let ourselves be this open vessel. We keep telling ourselves how much trouble being so dreamy and strange has caused us. Because dropping into this level goes against what we have learned to do, it takes a desperate conviction to make it work.

What we ultimately come to inside the Fourth House is a rededication, a recommitment. We offer up our personality structures into searing fires. We start again. Not to be hooked on outside patterns is to be a foundationally free being. To claim this freedom is to enter upon a different lifetime within this one.

What will the free lifetime be like? Determined to see everybody through the planetary crisis, we will put ourselves into whatever needs us in an Earth-alive fashion. We will tap those past lives that have the most to show us. Linking up with our future lives, we will prepare for them solely by becoming aligned with our deepest instincts from this time forth.

Most poignantly, the free lifetime in the Fourth House will meet each other soul from the deep inside, discarding all the trappings.

Where we were not met, we will now do the meeting. What we weren't given will be realized whenever *anybody* needs a place to be.

Pisces

Pisces is not who she is. The fish who makes her way through the world is put there to please and placate, keeping everybody happy. It is the other fish who is the true Pisces. She is the one who sends her sister out into the world to make sure that she herself will be left alone.

The other fish lives in so many places. She is a shape-changer. She is good at contriving fishes to fit each worldly game. She keeps on shifting, moving, becoming. The other fish travels on the interior. She joins the dead, the angels, and all others who are staying tuned. That is really what the other fish does — she stays tuned.

Let us now move all the way inside the other fish. Let us do the impossible. Let us imagine, conceive, journey into where the other fish is at home. We will need to leave behind us our separative egos and pick them up later. This is intuitive territory and it's been a long time since we've known our way there. But here we go anyway.

We are travelling through the threshold. It is thin and permeable. Any and all worlds are here. We wander along their edges. Whichever way we go, here we are, partaking of infinity. All sensations flood through us. We are moving toward the place we are meant to go. This journey has been unfolding for a long time. But we are starting to find our way.

There is a Presence inside of us, deep in this body. It is more who we are than we are ourselves. We have seen its intimations in the first three houses and their planets and signs. The houses in fact build on each other; they are really the same house in different cosmic positions. We are all incarnate in the same world. Each house in this sequence thus reflects the potentials and dilemmas of the previous ones while adding a tiny twist or ounce of energy, a quantum loop to them.

We act out an empirical ego, but that is just something to play with.

Here, inside, we are Christ; we are whole Spirit; we are Something Always Known. As the Piscean presence breaks through, our navigational feelers switch to "alert"; we can sense that we are inside of something mighty, that there is a purpose to our wanderings, and that we are indeed called.

Even as we enter upon this mystery, it is so familiar, so resonant. How many times have we crossed over the threshold and met the one who awaits us? How many times have we tapped the Deeper Presence, the Universal Force? And how many times have we tried to stay in this, only to be tossed about once again?

Pisces is the one who bears a tale, a myth, a memory stream that goes way back. The Pisces who lives a life is just a fragment. Pisces herself is harboring, nurturing, fostering something on the inside that can never be limited to any form, structure, or pattern. All of evolution is bursting into what has been missing; it is able to center enough to believe in itself, know itself, stay with itself, even as a bottomless turbulence tests the soul so many times over. Pisces is the dream that we forgot, yet the dream does not forget itself.

Just automatically, even while going deep in, we deprive ourselves of the great bulk of our needs. We float into tasks, cycles, relationships which use us up. We indulge ourselves in strange habits, ways of making very little of what we really bear. It is as though the shadow were monolithic and massive and knew how to stop us cold better than any part of us knew how to stay clear and true.

It is this harrowing level of soul experience by which Pisces typically defines itself. We wish, yet we do not do what we wish. We seek, but we condemn our seeking. We stand against ourselves. What is this shadow towering above us (and more than traumatic)?

Pisces is doing battle on a daily basis with the Lord of Death. This means that an exceedingly harsh and barren energy-frequency tries to suck all the life out of the Piscean soul. This frequency has a relentless fury to it, masking itself as cold strategic logic and implacable will. It is this horrendous layer that so often takes charge. Pisces must access sufficient Cosmic goodness and inner light to neutralize and even overcome the workings of evil, the machinations of cleverness and worldly cunning.

Wherever each one is weakest and most susceptible, Pisces has a personal version of this traumatic life or death struggle to enact. The only remedy is to build up inner strength precisely where one feels virtually helpless. Pisces cannot indulge secret pockets of negativity and get away with it.

The beauty of Pisces is that in the thick of ancient battles and harrowing ordeals, there arises a heart force, a soul depth with willingness and capacity to be aware and selfless. The very worst passages and cycles may yield the most inwardly renewing of touchstones. The greatest wounds may beget a near-immortal ability to embody, to hang in here, never to be ripped away from what really counts.

Pisces yearns for Heaven, the Cosmos, the Divine, for the intangible and unknown. The very best expression of Pisces is to be willing to be in exile from the Divine while still opening one's soul to search and longing. Only by our missing something, by needing it badly enough, by knowing that this is all that will sustain the soul will a foundational grace be restored.

The wonder of Pisces is that she is so self-giving, even when she feels there is nothing left to offer. Becoming vehicle, a vessel, Pisces can allow greater energy awareness when it is needed. Pisces' fruition is to awaken one's own core flame, being there as well within oneself. The ancient timeless faculties are something for the future. The testings have done their part. The soul is ready to embrace its own essence, to unite with the soul of the world, to be here at last.

The infinite Piscean mystery is that many roads lead to the very same place. All it takes is crazy perseverance to make each path yield true fruits. You cannot go wrong. You can delay the inevitable. But the destination is always luminously in view.

Pisces needs to unite the personal and the universal, to fuse her own story with the whole of evolution. This convergence opens a path for all to follow. When the one inside is the same as every world one meets, the last barrier dissolves, and we are here together as one.

The Moon

The most intimate, personal, unquestioned facet of selfhood we will ever move through is the Moon. She indwells the subtle fluids, the oceans, the cellular feelers—every place where there is a world within a world, a deeper circle embedded inside an outer, self-evident one. The Moon accompanies us through our every cycle and passage. She watches over us, makes sure we take up what is ours to experience, to process, to move through, to identify within. The Moon is certain that, if we take up a personal soul journey, we will be able to make our own way through life.

Yet the Moon is the most polarized and contradictory of all planetary influences—for she represents just as sharply the power of giving ourselves away, of losing ourselves completely. Her counter-instinct leads her to merge within contexts indiscriminately. She wants to pour through, to be tapped by life in whatever way life needs her to be. This pathway is dangerous—for, if the cycle and the occasion converge in the right compulsive combination, the Moon will instantaneously surrender everything she has built up over quite some time.

The Moon is friend and lover, adviser and orchestrator, the one who does it all. Her wisdom is variable. When she is on, in phase, in tune, she bears intact a textured knowingness that is capable of shepherding us through the tightest predicaments with barely a scratch. This knack or touch is what she counts on. In its peak times, the Moon can easily assist and mediate the passage we are needing to take up, and she will bring us there in style. For the Moon delights sensuously in the challenge of steering through hard places, turning around absurd dilemmas, making struggle and loss into the basis for new life. Willing and available, the Moon will always tell you how she feels, what she senses, and what is likely to happen next. At her best she is quite a stunning performer and companion.

However, the Moon is notoriously moody—or perhaps really just impressionable to many subtle influences and dynamics. Her voice just as convincing and ardent as ever, she rarely recognizes when she is off. In many life situations, the Moon will identify reality with anybody-but-self and will value the inner soul almost not at all. Liking to release what she has held too tight, the Moon can especially strongly be influenced by strong exterior forces. She gets easily intimidated or impressed, or perhaps vicariously identified with those who are colorful and dramatic.

Most of us are captured by our own Moon's enchantments, spells, trances. We have preferences and desires, characteristic longings and dreams, phobias and obsessions. While we also can be as clear and on the beam as the highest gods could ever wish for us, we usually fall for the same thing every time. Seldom do we stand objective to our Moon. We sink with her and rise with her—and we feel fatalistically stuck and passively given over to this position.

Our vision is the highest frequency of the Moon. It involves gathering all our foundational soul impressions into one thematic whole. We become a sense organ for the Earth and for all-that-is. We can see, feel, know truly. In the place of vision, we are shown, are led by spirit; our Moon then rests in the good hands of the angels.

A more characteristic place for the twentieth-century Moon to hang out has been the soul depths, most of which are experienced subjectively as happening to us from the outside or from unknown sources. As a psychic undertow takes hold of us, we are supply molded by these interstices. As in other planets, we become our world in all its subconscious traps and hiding places. We drift, wander, and lose center. Many factors imprint themselves within us—the vivid and repetitive images and characters of our dream self. We do not know our way in, through, or out. We seem to be cast in place as part of the way everything flows.

Our Moon is doing everything in her power to bring us to life and to help us to bring others to life. Sometimes she acts in crude and ineffective ways—but her intent is to bring us home to Earth and to the body. She is very persistent in her attempts to find the best way to do this.

What we can explore through our Moon's guidance is the path of surrendering ourself to life's graces and to spirit's call. This is a tricky endeavor—for we may give over to what seems like life's graces, portrays itself as spirit's call, yet is anything but. The Moon must learn the hard way, through lots of experience, where reality lies, likewise where illusion takes her.

The ultimate message of our Moon is that we must come down from our lofty heights—our mental abstractions—and rediscover the arts of living. She passionately introduces us (once again) to a power that lives in nature, that imbues Earth with a primal depth charge. She takes us for many rides in the vicinity of intimacy, caring, and fellow feeling, for she knows this is where we have lost much of late; this is where we need a perpetual refresher course.

The Moon wishes us to be more like tribal ancients and future visionaries and less like mechanics or those playing remote-control mind games. She hatches in us a craving for the thing which satisfies the inner soul. She throws off all that is alien, controlling, superimposed, counter-feeling.

In a simple everyday way, our Moon locates us firmly inside a physical body, inside spaces and energies which are palpable and definite. She will teach us how to honor and be within what is most basic and right-here. The Moon clothes herself in that which is home-grown, familiar, old-fashioned, forever known.

The one thing you can count on is that the Moon, in all its soul moods, will be there dancing its destiny dance. And since we never can get away from it, our best chance is gracefully to become the Moon and all the while recognize that we have fallen for something that is our very own.

Pluto

Pluto awakens us inside the world dream. It is often a very rude comeuppance with a sting and a bite. Slowly we lose everything we had, everybody we thought we were. And then we are void, empty. If we can stay within the void self, a whole new phase of our existence will follow—one that will be more than worth our agonies of awakening.

Most of us have dwelled a long time far removed from the subterranean places through which Pluto needs to bring us—so we sense the initial impact of Pluto taking us over and exposing us to strange locales and volatile energies. There is actually more than one Pluto that we can encounter. There is the Lord of Death Pluto, and then there is one to whom we come when we are no longer under the power of the Lord of Death.

The Lord of Death Pluto occupies the popular imagination, seizing our fresh soul, dragging us into the Underworld, and forcing us to live there as captives. He treats us as though we belong to Him and to nobody else. In fact, he won't let us be in touch with anybody or anything, except for *his* forces. He tries to talk us into adopting the harshest and grimmest and most surreal world as what is real, inescapable, and the hidden truth behind all lovely appearances. The Lord of Death is after our soul.

There is also another Lord of the Underworld. When we are not death-bound, not caught in the shadow of previous deaths, not afraid to face mortality and immortality, we are given over to a foundational Plutonian influence. This one is truly liberating. It too starts as a fiery cauldron that takes away what we were bound up within, but the core Pluto is benevolent, seeking to access our deepest resources and spring us from our old traps. It is not always easy to discern which Pluto is which. But if we are in the core Pluto journey, our root self will arise and bless the passage of the planet.

Any and all Plutonian influences work to loosen our grip upon our personal separative self, in order to quicken our pulse of attention to something beyond us that we dwell at the center of—something very different from the stuff we generate on our own. The infernal Plutonian influence draws us unfailingly toward solitary confinement within an infinite existence that mocks us. The redemptive Pluto removes our insulations and gives us true fusion with everything in this world that claims us as New Earth citizen.

The Plutonian decades, since 1930 (with its outward scientific discovery), have been leading us into a new alignment with the Etheric

Christ, the Living Christ in the Clouds. This involves a complete internalization of the Christ, a way to make Him our core self. When we are aligned with the Christ Within Us, our world changes its feeling tone and psychic charge. Let us now view what this is really all about.

Our ordinary self-identification has been within the lunar enclaves. We are the ancestors through whom we came. We are the collective that surrounded us as we grew. We are past lives radiating inside, karmically compelling and full of lingering issues—and we are the adaptations we make as we grapple with our soul fate within a naively immediate sense experience.

The Christ Within Us becomes a Plutonian presence that shifts the energy frequency within and then just as strongly outside us. We enter into a communion with the Earth's soul— a thing which arises within our own deeper center. The ongoing conversation between the Earth's soul and our own deep center builds a grail quest *into* this life, not so much personally as from an awakening planetary center. This awakening force is all-pervasive, turning around what was most personal and narrowly enclosed. It targets wherever we were clannish, habitual, blinded. The Christ Plutonian Presence lights a deep and enduring fire under us. We catch the blaze of how the Earth is awakening within her own soul.

In the most exquisite characteristic of the Christ Self, we meet Christ in each one of us equally. It is not for the elect, the true believers; it is something that impresses itself through each one's soul life. We sense it and draw it forth wherever we find it. Something starts to spread, something that is passionately alive and mutually empowering.

If we persist in awakening within the Christ Self, we become both volatile and consoling, both revolutionary and evolutionary. Our energy disrupts patterns that have outlived their usefulness. Yet we are right there with the inner soul of each and the inner soul of the whole situation.

The innermost truth of the Plutonian Presence is, in order to be a good channel for everybody to see and know themselves through, we have been thrown free of purely personal fear and anxiety. The absence of personal shadow qualities tests us quite a bit—for we must stay within situations saturated with negative undercurrents. We must not polarize, reject, or demonize what we encounter.

Our path now becomes stripped bare to only one thing. We ask spirit to stream through us and bring its gifts, our own part being co-creative, yet also deeply surrendered. We know now that we are to be spirit-bearers in each and every situation, but this fact reveals itself often not at all in a traditional spiritual vein. The Plutonian domain seeks no trappings, no familiar symbolisms. It wants to get down to it and stay down.

We will never emerge from the Plutonian frequencies. They will keep guiding us further down in. But as we get good at being aware in the depths, the Christ Presence will sit within us serenely and effortlessly. Pluto in the end is not so hard, not so strange. It's simply being one with the remotest planet in a true sense. Whatever it takes to get there, Pluto will bring us. Lots of death. Many shatterings. Yet it turns out saturated with love, beaming a very pure, fine light from very faraway. Pluto is master of disguises, revealer of essences. But isn't that how it should be for the tiniest planet in the farthest orbit, bearing down on us from the longest and most cosmic fulcrum within the Solar System.

We are on a Plutonian track nowadays, all of us, to the end.

The Fifth Life Stream

The Fifth House

Being in this body in this world is not a given. It is a task and a journey. The Fifth House offers us the finest accommodations along our own individual incarnational tour. Yet to carry through each step of the path of life and death every living moment is arduous. We confront that within ourselves which cannot go on at every turn, and still we are asked to keep the momentum moving forward, as we become the world, become the core of life.

We are operating under conditions of karmic theater. Just like the best of actors or actresses, we need to become the part, to feel that protagonist's hidden feelings, to track closely what is sparking them into being. Concentrating on being our best self is the first layer of the performance. Though many of us won't deepen beyond this stage, there are several stages still to go.

At the stage of the best self, we sense the dramatic spotlight of our life's destiny commanding an exemplary performance. Through ourselves we wish to reveal how it is meant to be done—so we are "on" much of the time. We have "routines," though we think of them as just ourselves. We can be generous and loving, expansive and life-generative. We especially delight in being applauded, being seen, being surrounded by acclaim. We sense this as vital to our well being. It is our connection to the world itself. It not only confirms our acts, it gives us acts.

What takes us beyond this point?

For one, we are catalyzed when things don't work out as we planned. Though we generate a tremendous amount of effort and striving, hard work and dedication, a given stage of life fails to catch fire. Laboring rather than being truly ourselves, subject to the manifold outer effects that take charge here, we no longer know who to be or why. Without further ado this situation can disintegrate into crises and false trails. As it does, we pass into the second stage of the Fifth House life wave where we find ourselves dwelling in shadows. The suppressed and denied assert themselves and command a central prospect, riveting our attention; we grapple anew with our own reflections.

Spectral chords binding the soul in the body from deep underneath turn us into what we fear, what we suspect is most wrong, what we remember inextricably (from elsewhere) as our chronic syndromes. We are more than stuck. Along a subterranean route, past-life selves, their stories, their abandonments, their deaths, their incompletions rearise, for they are lodged deep inside of us. These become tightly linked with our early life patterns, parental and childhood authorities, and with the key figures of our lives now. The chords bind us such that we cannot liberate our core selves and let be. Whether as complete experience or undertone, this pulse sends us along a depth cycle of the journey. We know as we descend into the mist that we shall not return the same.

Becoming aware of our subtler underlying blocks and resistances is a process that is still new among creatures in the Earth's collective evolution. Most of the methods and approaches they take never scrape bottom. Yet to fathom the measure of one's own madness, one's self-entanglement, is the greatest journey anyone ever undertakes.

The second shadow stage of the Fifth House is marked by King Lear wandering in a lonely heath, making too much sense for his own well-being and too little sense to others. We drop down far under, where we meet everybody who has awaited us. The degree of our descent during this venture sets the fiber of the third stage.

When we truly get into the underbelly, we bear the fruits of our depth journey. We become legitimately present to ourselves. To live this way is satisfying and fulfilling enough to motivate us mightily to get there. It is a great moment in the karmic theater when the central performer is no longer directed toward how they seem, but instead focused on the vibrant essence of their true self. This unfolds in each soul in a mysterious individual pattern that nobody can predict or control.

Then what happens?

The props are removed from on stage. Dramatic action diminishes mysteriously. A Presence of spirit magnitude starts to fill the atmosphere. Nobody is here; everybody is here.

The fun begins. In the third stage of the Fifth House, we create a reality that is a true home for ourselves and those we love. We carve out and craft a space from within. As our body is becoming the vessel that will take us across, we at last dig deep roots and make our peace with who we are and with our world as a whole. We are new again.

A rare fourth stage can be described as following the Christ Within at such a faithful level that the entire karmic theater dissolves. Without any further heavy substance to be bound up within we find ourselves here in Earth as we are in Spirit Realms. While holding us fast, the microcosm liberates us, moves with us. We are the world reborning.

No matter which stage of the Fifth House we are travelling—whether one of them or a combination of them at a given time: we share this one central sensibility. We are drawn in this house to make room for creative individuality; in fact, far more room than is commonly allocated. What we want to see and become is a true self, a meaningful force, a being who can embody creative individuality with fervor, gusto, and panache. We can't settle for a pale imitation. The one who emerges as self here is invested with the magical power of charisma, a specially charged destiny, a brilliant aura and poise. This is something we cannot lightly push away—for here we know indelibly that the entity we come to in ourselves is the point of life, that all else follows from its central radiance.

Through excesses, ego abuses, affectations—a legion of patterns—everything in this house is magnified, including its distortions and shortcomings. In characteristic ways we pretend, fantasize, perform even in solitary. It is not easy to be charged from inception with an extra dimension of self-consciousness and self-awareness—but most essentially the Fifth House is where we show what wool we are made of and what we can knit of it at our utmost capacity—or else we feel the brunt of falling short and know we must concede. We are left supporting in others fiercely what we ourselves missed.

Leo

Each sign of the zodiac is formed perfectly from within itself to be just what it needs to be. Yet Leo takes this course to the furthest extent it can be taken. Leo seals off everything that is alien or strange, corking *in* what suits, what feels to be one's own world, one's own self, one's style, one's very substance. She then proceeds to put her individual stamp or imprint upon everything in the vicinity. For Leo must be Leo.

What follows from this prerogative and priority is a need that depends upon one central quality of character—a quality so definitive along the Leo pathway that everything comes to pivot, over and again, around it. To wield power and influence rightfully, Leo must develop a truly selfless self. A merely self-filled self (of the usual kind) is poison for Leo. The one sign most susceptible to the petty ego must overcome it or else be at the mercy of every whim, each habit of that ego—must overcome it or become it. A hampered Leo becomes mired in primally entangled layers of selfhood.

Developing a selfless self, incarnating it realistically, is a karmic journey of the utmost intensity. You can't get there unless you act out and move through each facet and fragment of the self-filled self first. You can't avoid it just because it's unevolved or in the way. This is sacred vow, the resolution to be true that by itself gets you through. Finally fathoming is far more painful than glorious. The inner core self continually cries out that this particular phase in which we have caught her is dangerously off, not where either of us wants to go, not what everybody needs us to be.

According to twentieth-century criteria, Leo should be getting away with it and having a great time. Of course, many a Leo will try in precisely this way to simulate what is expected. But if anything drives the self crazy, it is being momentarily at the mercy of a personal arbitrary self that it knows is more destructive and temporary than really who it is. The path of least resistance splits between two highly divergent layers of selfhood—the one under and the one over live two different lives. Standard fare, this model is extremely hard to dislodge once it settles. Here we find the secret torment in the Leonine path of development.

With a stunning ability to make them look and seem fascinating, compelling, inescapable, the over self plays out all current fantasies of selfhood. Torrents of life force and phosphors of consciousness are given over to manifesting outwardly a mere prototype, an archetype, a performance nonetheless magnificent. Despite typical hopes and dreams that this will be enough, it never is. Yet if the over self is sufficiently impressive, nobody will look any closer, including one's own under self.

The under self hides in the unconscious mind, hanging down there indefinitely. This Leo under self is formidable, vast, unquenchably negative. Dwelling inside depression and despair, it maintains a complete shadow of what the over self is exuding. It most characteristically generates a self-critique, a self-judgment that is bleak, fatalistic, and thoroughly convinced of its own sarcastic read-out of the situation at hand.

The relationship between the over self and the under self determines most everything along the Leo pathway. Integrating their polar expressions alone leads to a true capacity to discover the selfless self within. In the worst-case scenario, over and under self split off from each other and develop vast worlds apart, as completely out of communication as continents separated for millennia by oceans. Such a split tends to be deep and foundational.

However, there is also good news along the Leo track. From a spiritual vantage point, Leo is the most gifted and blessed of signs—and this side of things comes into play at every juncture in hidden, significant ways. Leo is not on his or her own. Spiritual guiding forces feed strongly into each Leo lifetime. They select what is vital and essential, casting off the rest. Whenever a Leo is able to collaborate wakefully with spirit inspiration and infusion, a quite different pathway unfolds. In recent times, this hyperdimensional infusion has become far more prevalent and accessible.

The axis on which the spiritual journey of Leo pivots is that of the Above and the Below. The interior quest of Leo is vertically aligned, a requirement to walk in balance and integration. This requires deep roots and high expanded faculties. As this ultimate dimension unfolds, the selfless self—the Christ Within—becomes a natural expression, an embodied presence in the midst of life.

Even along this projectile, many fragmentary domains refuse to cooperate with the Greater Design. Leo has an inveterate tendency to miss key factors during her journey, and these accumulate as problem areas. The brighter the light along the Leo pathway, the more wildly dissonances proliferate. Leo must learn to take responsibility not just for what is perceived, but for what is missed. The burden of Leo is the neglected and denied.

Leo's imperative is to penetrate through self to Greater Self, to navigate astoundingly precipitous shoals into a boundless sense of rightfulness. It is also to strip the over self of its manic acting-out impulses, while simultaneously freeing the under self of its depressive convictions and morbid assumptions. It takes great depth of character and immense perseverance to become a Leo truly; yet it is clear to those who watch the Leo path that every juncture is overflowing with gifts and treasures.

Leo fosters and sustains a thousand special touches and carings, endowing the Earth with something extra, something it might otherwise never have. Leo's gifts are always there. The generative characteristics of Leo are simply awesome. Even a Leo that is off confers more benefits than most other signs when they are on—for Leo is the master of life expression in all facets from birth unto death and beyond.

To embrace and accept with no qualifications and conditions one's own core nature is Leo's ultimate task. Once you can do it all, it's hard to be reconciled to any detached part of it. When Leo smiles on the inside, the world is utterly renewed. Toward this eventuality, we all raise our toast to the best health and good spirits of our Leo friends.

Saturn

Saturn is what we become exiled and estranged from when we take on the mental construct of "the outer world counts and the inner world is no business of ours." You can't do Saturn meaningfully from the outside; yet, conversely, there is no starry influence more frequently worked from the surface than Saturn.

The Saturn we know is not the real one. The real Saturn that we have pushed far away from us is the one we don't know how to approach any longer. Let us tarry a while over the socialized Saturn and then investigate what the Other One wishes to reveal.

The socialized Saturn is so familiar and commonplace that we must step several paces back from it to see it at all. Saturn generally holds each one tightly to outward obligations, literal form requirements. These are obeyed as a superstructure—what makes civilization possible. Thus, each one is talked into the proposition that what applies to everybody must apply to them. It becomes self-evident here that we must do our duty, serve the world around us first, and ask questions later—if later ever comes.

The hidden clauses in this contract are killers. Any facet of our personal soul that will impede societal Saturn's crucial tasks and objectives must of course be pushed under and kept under. Whoever within us sees differently, knows a different reality from this one is treated as our inner enemy and renounced. But it is no good if we only do it to ourselves. We try to stamp out these same qualities in others and in the world around us. We must be sure to help each and every one to do as we are doing, to become the perfect citizen of the Old World Order.

The ills of this jamboree compound upon themselves. Layer upon layer of self-discounting vie for the dubious privilege of keeping the world going in outermost style. Because this role and its associated tasks are the most rewarded ones in the whole surface world's infrastructure, its bounties are irresistible, its advantageousness indisputable.

In a deeper sense, the greater distortion involved here is that once you have trained yourself and conditioned yourself to operate in this fashion, your attempts to overthrow the condition of the socialized Saturn will be greatly hobbled and delayed. And so many times over, you will convince yourself that you have indeed conquered the socialized Saturn, only to find later that you are lapsing into yet another variant on the same theme.

The hardest force in the world to overcome is the socialized Saturn. It sinks its roots and teeth into flesh. Dislodging it, uprooting it needs guts and self-conviction. And Saturn robs us of all self-conviction long before we get to this point. It seems like a prison you can't escape from, a way of life you have no way meaningfully to intend to put behind you, not given how this world works.

The last image we can grab hold of in the socialized Saturn world is the collective realization that because this hollowed Saturn is indeed devouring the common soul of our times, each one of us has a critical internal imperative now to free ourselves from the monster, first inside our whole self and then in whatever domain of society calls us. There can be no more urgent work than this.

The rigid authority of those in charge is a retrogressive power which our inner, true Saturn is here to dispute, to contend with, and to get to the bottom of, with the goal of eventually being done with it altogether. The same planet we hold responsible for our most ingrained negative patterns of behavior can be transmuted into the one planet capable of drastically espying through and slashing every facet of the false world system and the terms of our enslavement in it. However, to tap the true Saturn is to descend into a dark inner place; it is to withdraw from all scapegoating of the enemy, all projection of evils to the outside; it is to plunge into the actual molten lava of how we do this to ourselves. Saturn is the ultimate karmic planet. We don't escape it by velocity or flight; we escape it only by becoming it, by passing through it into something else, a something else that is what it truly is.

The stuff we have learned to do here is usually the same stuff we have done to ourselves in similar ways since well before we could ever recover memory. We've been falling under socialized Saturn for hundreds and thousands, and even hundreds of thousands, of years.

A starkly ingrained pattern serves its hedonism and appetites for the status quo by relegating the outside to conventional and acceptable package deals of a quite delicious self, while keeping on the inside the severe and harsh inner critic who hates living this way, all the time shuttling back and forth feverishly between these two points in order to keep the outer going and the inner on ice. Since this takes a pressurized, stressful, high-energy output to maintain, we can't let the façade down for a moment.

The true Saturn, of course, is more than a menial critic; she knows that there is nothing to this syndrome, in self or others—that in every nuance it is manufactured, manipulated, controlled. She can dismantle anything that has been put together, however brutally and implacably, because its fabrication is only from the outside. All it takes is our willingness to get down to where these syndromes have taken root inside us, and using crazy wisdom to bust them up—long before the world outside has given us the go-ahead to do so.

A cosmic Saturn is always imbedded within the true Saturnian framework. This indestructible core has witnessed, with fascination and dread, our falling under a socialized Saturn banner. This core bears an intact alternative, ready to go, not the least bit impressed or daunted by what has happened previously or its hegemony and public relations.

This greater Saturn reveals that the separative ego has merely been hiding behind the infinite excuse of doing what everybody is doing; its attachment and identification are strictly with the outer self and its needs and demands. Socialized Saturn is a mask for self-absorbed Saturn to strike a good deal and keep on bargaining—but it's actually a rotten deal, and the stakes are now so high that we must call in the cosmic Saturn to clean up our act.

When Saturn is true and cosmically founded, it bears the one specific characteristic that is its saving grace—Saturn is rooted in ancient origins of the world and forged by the backbone of human evolution. What it knows and bears is the timeless wisdom we used to and soon shall (once again) take as our touchstone for each breath of life. This timeless wisdom asserts with pristine clarity that inside we are still untouched, untapped, waiting—still longing. All that we are has not even broken a sweat yet. Our real story is about to begin.

Earth Under

Precisely opposite the Sun in each one's star pattern stands the Earth. This is the Earth Shadow, the Earth Under. It represents and embodies what we have discarded, what we have lost, what we have died to—that part within us that is compost. The Earth Under is the core of self we seek to put behind us, to be done with permanently. The thing that kills us over and over again, the Earth Under gathers like iron filings all sub-earthly imaginations of being consumed by life, being abused and forced out. Whatever we are furthest from in our current life direction and most deeply haunted by will show up in our Earth Under position as something to be engaged yet one final time and reduced to ashes permanently.

Most of us do not have much of an idea what to do with our Earth Under, for it hardly surfaces at all. We find it easy to sweep it away from us, meet it only in the darkest facets of what we most fear and avoid. Perhaps it is wise for those who are seeking security and safety to steer clear of the Earth Under. Even for those who can take the journey into the Earth Under successfully, there remains one strong caution sign. When you directly confront the full scope of your Earth Under, when you return to the surface, you will be so different that you will never again belong to the company of those who avoid this place.

Let us say that, in a particular case, recent deaths in recent lifetimes have been repeatedly and repetitively traumatic. Perhaps a situation was set up in such a way that one had to run into oneself at the very end of each lifetime, yet was unable to move into what was revealed. From these successional events there arises in this lifetime an unconscious Earth Under position which successfully eludes any and all attempts to get at it. A soul persisting in going in there anyway is proclaiming on inner levels it is seeking to reverse, here and now, all recent lifetimes. It is trying to break the one pattern that doesn't seem like a pattern at all, but is assumed to be "it," "this," "once and forever."

The battle is joined. One's own death-guardian stands before the self. This herald will not permit a full-scale realization of what is cooking deep under until satisfied that the current-time self, lit up by the Sun (as only the Sun can burnish), has a *real* chance to slay the ghost of the past. Often this means many initial attempts thwarted. When readiness is demonstrated, the entire underlying tale becomes revealed.

It is likely that the outcome of this battle will hinge upon whether one can defeat death itself. To meet a pattern of past deaths squarely is to be directly inside the deeper shadow, the one we flee in our darkest nightmares. What we tend to fight is the very fact that in past lives our soul sought refuge in death to keep from being forced to stay with the excruciating self-quest.

In modern times, so many deaths are self-inflicted secretly. We want out of here, out of the struggle, but the struggle is all there is, so we may get out of "here," but we don't get out of the struggle. Whenever you come up against any form of suicide in your soul's record, you are at the crux point of your ultimate earthly battle.

Viscerally, this feels like being ripped apart at the roots, being ripped further and further beyond endurance and needing to learn to surrender into rent-asunder energetics. You have to sense in slow motion what it really meant to the soul in the past (in some form of desperate impulse) to abandon its Earthly home. It is hard to be at once fully down under there and yet somehow dispassionate, refusing to turn this reincarnational experience against oneself now, yet again.

In a sense, the self in present time must rescue itself from the fate in past time of once again losing one's life to doubts and fears. This rescue must be fully authentic. As you drown in your own past creations, you emerge breathing heavily on shore because this time you stayed with yourself. The one who dies by suicide dissolves into the ethers quite fast, missing his or her death altogether. Dying one's undied previous deaths is the direct route to move from pervasive dis-empowerment to lasting self-empowerment.

We bear still with us the stark evidence of where we got the most lost in life and death. We are beginning to develop the resources that will be needed to reverse the flow of feeling called to repeat the syndrome of losing the self in worlds after worlds through which we can no longer make our way, at least in any viable fashion.

When we return from the reckoning with our own past weaknesses and susceptibilities, for the first time our Solar energy-wave will have muscle, weight, substantive backup. When we say something then, we will mean it. When we do something, the thing will cash in. When we seek at last to be true to ourselves, the path will be open and clear.

The Sun no longer shadowed by the Earth, we cease to generate karmas everywhere we go. We no longer snare ourselves. Best of all, now we give life in abundance without destroying who we are in the process.

To cut through the Earth Shadow is to imagine and conceive that every layer of human experience lives inside of us somewhere and is calling out, crying out to be cleared. We track our reactions as sheer clues. It is a given that wherever our buttons get pushed the hardest and most frequently is where we have gotten bound up within an Earthbound state. This is the state that we must free ourselves from if we wish to walk this incarnation upright.

The Earth Under sobers and humbles absolutely everybody. It reveals unfailingly that the counter-image of the ideal self is alive and well deep inside. Because we can transform this inward darkness, its pull is immense. Once you tune into it, you find that the Earth Under has been shouting at the top of its lungs every day of your life, every night too. Hearing it and responding to its pleas is a great mercy and the start of a journey we will never forget again.

The Sixth Life Stream

The Sixth House

Just below the surface of ordinary affairs, what we could call the subconscious mind works through and processes straightforward daily events and experience with such intensive activity that it would seem there is something more to our outward preoccupations than we imagine. The outer mind, presumably conscious, tells itself all the time that facts are facts, that what you see is what you get. Yet the subtler mind underneath is even more active, convinced that everything is what you make it, that there are multiple realities, and that the best way to handle this situation is to pretend to be as flat and straightforward as possible, while working the territory fully with all one's deeper powers.

Overtly manifesting myriad details of outer everyday functioning, the Sixth House tracks closely the semblance level—whether it is the physical body's health and well-being, adaptations and survival necessities amidst daily work, or just keeping every factor juggling in relation to every other. Any and all of these are simply what we all must deal with as conscious adults.

Life provides complications, conflicts of interest and attention, and endless other matters to work out. Technology causes this multiplicity to snowball; urban life evinces several distinct worlds at once. Under these conditions the overt manifestation of the Sixth House becomes quite a field to master. Yet all of this is actually a front. While the outer mind is mechanical and routine— habitually setting up many automatic and reflexive activity streams, the subconscious mind—barely detected, not granted its pivotal role—is doing its magic.

The Sixth House changes with the times. Its outer expression is adaptive, accommodating, flexible to what is demanded and required at every turn. Its subconscious aspect shifts even more, always a bit ahead of the game, striving to gain sufficient leverage to be able to understand the hidden factors and motivations which make up real human interchange.

The subconscious networker moves from under to under, not surface to surface. He or she in us becomes fine-tuned in psychological skills and interactional dynamics. Contrary to our suspicions, the networker *does* seek to co-create, to collaborate, to find a common ground for mutual support and encouragement.

The networker knows that the world is wide open, that each situation evolves as we respond to cues that come our way. She witnesses multiple channels of future-soaked existence as stimulating, pleasurable, promising, offering hope, generous with opportunities. She is adept in the art of playing it cool on the surface, while inwardly heating up with movements that allow her to tap the flow of events.

Our subtle mind seeks optimal convergence between collective forces and the individual need to expand capacity. To implement such a vision, a tireless networking activity is generated, most of it beyond the scope of outer exertion and tangible factors. Such layers show up as dreams and body symptoms; we dream our world to be what it is for us inside. The layers spread from there into runaway imagination, a driving force to be somebody, a charged search for a context, support system, open arena within which to operate synchronously.

While the cover-up outer mind keeps claiming security, stability, comfort—whatever is most reassuring and normal, the immensely potent inner mind seeks innovation, stretching and expanding its dimensions.

The collective mind has been dragging behind the probings and discoveries of each one's subtle mind for a long time, so the networker inside of us must be facile with both styles and semblances. We go outside into bland gestures, inwardly networking feverishly for life and change.

Playing the edge this way keeps our Sixth House planets busier than any others. They are tapped for everything they've got. We want them to perform to outer specifications, to generate a new world all the while.

We must serve two masters. Convenience of outer form dictates customary and traditional formality. Urgencies of inner process compel us toward radical revitalization at every level at once. This combination gets our attention, mobilizes our powers.

As we head into a different world, the split is starting to narrow. The polar worlds are coming together. What we've been working on forever inside, just out of sight, is reaping dividends. Stuck patterns are revealing their vital currency. Nothing remains as it was when artificial outer stability, seemingly forever, held sway.

In a regime of changes fast and furious, the Sixth House is the best place to be. We set the networker to work and it spins the multi-colored cloth of future worlds, a tapestry far more bountiful and elegant than the flat twentieth century seemed to promise.

Aquarius

The sign of Aquarius is illuminated from within itself by a central vision, a motivating spark, an essential manifestation of powers and capacities of an extraordinary kind. Rarely are these seen clearly by the Aquarian herself. Instead, the vital springboard inside is taken as given and licensed to do what it does, to reveal its mysteries without much private selfhood. In Aquarius, the springboard prevails, the self serves the greater; proportion is restored; the universal way of things is uncovered.

Aquarius' idiosyncratic side is in evidence at close quarters. Aquarius does not simply embrace who one is, who the other is, and what is going on here. The outer mind of Aquarius is convinced that nothing is ever as it should be; we can always be doing better—trying harder, getting it right. The intricate details of what is daily perceived as being in the way could fill up every book in the world. The Aquarian shadow is that of the little mind, fooled and made to chase after phantoms everywhere. The outer mind of Aquarius does not get it and never will.

When vital matters are at hand, grace shifts Aquarius out of the little-mind mode. An immense universal flow sweeping her off her tight perch into unknown, open future territory, Aquarius finds she can turn to her springboard within for wisdom that will be there. This provenance is an evolutionary force available to all, yet it is usually Aquarians who initially bring it forth in a form that others can tap and identify with. Aquarius renders accessible the universal. When in flow, she is so commonsensically keen upon everyone tapping the universal springboard that it seems a simple matter of letting it through. And indeed it is.

Refinements are an essential factor with Aquarius. Even though the little outer mind is hopelessly hooked on semblances, and even while the inward awareness is ever ready to make way for the universal springboard with its expanded consciousness, it is actually the continuous intermingling of these two layers that characterizes the Aquarian path. It is difficult to keep these in their appropriate places and know when and how to move, make way, or keep it all going at every moment till the next curve unveils the pattern.

The biggest trouble comes from the separative ego in Aquarius' mental strategies. This ego tends to want to claim too much territory for itself, all the time self-oblivious, not seeing what it's doing. Ego mind can generate a very predictable rut of one's own narrow self-concepts. Outer-world facts and figures are misused to tyrannize and enslave the deeper soul, or at least keep its depths churned up and desperate to find outlet. The dull side of Aquarius does not know what to do with itself and busies itself forming a shield, an impenetrable barrier that soon hardens and crystallizes. Before Aquarius knows it, the most constrictive thought forms in the world have lodged themselves in one's cognitive field and begun to seem indispensable and inevitable.

Aquarius' path lies in outwitting one's own inward adversaries, the many voices of limitation, pragmatic reasoning, hard and fast logic and mental judgment. Strident and self-important, these voices surround and envelop the soul, clamoring and shouting, insisting upon their version of reality, their interpretation of facts. They become collective imprints.

When outer need and inner readiness come together, the ingenious and resourceful spirit of Aquarius alights. Aquarian expression at such a time is transparent to what is truly moving amongst us. To make such occasions a constant is a great art. Toiling in the mines of the outer ego-self does not necessarily vaunt one's own boundless abilities.

The most extraordinary manifestation of Aquarius is that good things can happen even when the inner soul is riddled by doubts and splits. Aquarians leverage their tension and self-struggles to feed their ability to be there for what arises, authentically giving substance to life, even as their own battle with the mind rages on as ever. That is what makes the deep Aquarian into an instrument of pop Aquarian culture.

The Aquarian brew is intoxicating. When it bubbles over, it sparks free space, persuasive appreciation, a vibration of resonance. Aquarius makes way for what is new and fresh and different, the further flung the better. Its understanding reveals a world of just-beginning-to-emerge factors and facets everywhere. Aquarius is the guardian of our shared future. Every fiber of Aquarius goes into making sure this level is not interfered with or stymied, is allowed to flourish in its own natural unfolding.

In deepest reality, Aquarius remains a welter of contradictions, of mutually ironically juxtaposed phenomena and attitudes. Nobody can put it all together. Nonetheless, the Aquarian gift is manifested at destiny moments when she gathers the most divergent ingredients toward their collective harvest. Blurs of changes within changes are Aquarian throughout. In times of stillness, something is masterfully being developed, being allowed to reveal itself. When we catch a glimpse, we see Aquarius right there, quietly attentive, making sure it *is* a new world.

Juno

As we have seen in the Vesta section of the Second Life Stream, each of the four main asteroids has functioned in the nineteenth and twentieth centuries as a goad, daring us to go ever further into the pathologies of the outer mind, the Earthbound will, and the fear-struck emotions. The asteroids have accompanied the final developments of the mass civilization and have simultaneously made it all much worse, thus made change in the entire system inevitable.

The asteroid Juno has been responsible for the comprehensive implementation of control mechanisms in the mass society. Its special province over the past two centuries has been to isolate a faculty of mind maintaining control over the subrational, irrational, or superrational aspect of life.

On a mental level, Juno harnesses what people do together from the vantage point of purely external surface factors. Therefore each one's Juno has been employed to standardize the self, to make it look and seem to be perfectly appropriate to the most conventional codes and ideas. This creeping compulsiveness has gone a lot further than we let ourselves know.

We have emphasized our meeker, more conformist side, and tapped our Juno to insist upon an outward problemless expression that nothing at all might disturb or call into question. Juno has done its job well. Everything is clean, clear, crisp, uncluttered, uncomplicated, and we are hopping about with outer pressures, forgetting inner depths and subtleties, detaining our potential.

These will be uprooting times for Juno, to neutralize her mental set of receiving this world hypersimplified as a given. She has gotten tightly patterned, hyper-literal, self-conscious. Shifting her out of the many layers of her paranoid trance will take committed hard work.

One's own negative convictions will be a persistent strain of self-sabotage. By believing the worst about ourselves and our world in a blind heedless fashion, we have Junoed ourselves, mentally and psychically, into a very tight corner. At first, all we can do is contest, argue, debate, consider alternatives, look at matters long and hard. We can turn Juno upon Juno. The task of talking ourselves out of our worst nightmares is a long, reiterative, and consuming one. Yet we cannot get around this priority. We will not find a new Juno until we have chased out of hiding the whole Juno complex of the nineteenth and twentieth centuries in our own individual variants.

Once we have achieved more of a neutral or truly objective vantage point, we can begin to find a Juno positive. We must develop the stance of being willing and available to foster humbly what is new and different, even before we feel it inside. Initially we simulate the behaviors of those who would operate that way. Then we discover that it makes sense to shift our weight of awareness from the negative and critical toward the progressive.

Juno shows what can happen as mass society breaks up its brittle patterns and engulfing syndromes. A series of steps arises, each one more firmly trooping into unknown territory and finding there a basis for hope and for further steps to be taken. We are using Juno now to accompany us in our transition from the prohibitive perspectives of old to the dawning vision of the unborn.

Juno positive is all about a skeptical, hard, and tough, yet vibrantly wide-open point of view on common affairs. We typically come to it through extreme crisis. Through long-term hard work on self we learn to say yes everywhere, where we always said no before.

The deeply practical advancing Juno makes room for myriad factors. She takes on tough, balky stuff, for she knows that only where her mix is sufficiently eclectic and attractive to new factors does evolution move as it can.

Our truth in Juno becomes an almost anonymous, somewhat generic participation in whatever is next on the collective agenda. As we are no longer entirely locked into how these things are reflected through media or manipulated voices, we are responsive to evolutionary cues, vibrating through culture and civilization everywhere—protean and multi-dimensional, beyond linear mind programs.

Juno is our bridging asteroid, leveraging us from the personal, individual to the common point of view. As she brims over with collective impressions, we need to shift these from outermost data and input to truth consciousness. Each one of us is in training through Juno for a New Earth coming. One of our first steps is to free ourselves from the tyranny of what has been stuffed down our throats for so long—every cynicism that has caught our devout attention in the past two centuries. What will happen when visions and original ideas supplant cynicisms? Will we learn to see the universe for ourselves at last?

The Seventh Life Stream

The Seventh House

We are very glad to be in the Seventh House. All of the first six houses have grounded us, gotten us ready, made us eager for what comes now.

What we meet here is ourselves, is another self we are drawn to. In the interplay between what lives in this self here and that other self we must find our way. The other self can be a part of ourselves with which we are deeply engaged—and it often is. Or it can be a spirit being, one of the dead, one of those we tap to guide and lead our soul's journey. But whoever the other is, we live for the full-scale interplay between the given one inside and the unknown self outside, the one who brings us news from afar.

The current that moves between self and other is a live-wire, full-blast circuit, one that will not leave us alone. Through that current we become more alive, far more deeply present to here. With that current activated, we can more fully flesh out existence in this world, in tandem with our cherished other.

Some of us can enter upon this intensive exploratory space with more than one soul, more than one other. When we enter with more than one soul, we expand our given biological nature toward futures that call for a multidimensional axis of sharing. Yet to live by multiple connections can only work if we become a truly vaster self in this body here and now. One way or the other, this prospect calls to us in our coupling and mating, mixing and matching. We want another. Nowadays, we want ourselves as well. Some of us want spirit presence as fully as the beloved other.

The primary thrust of the Seventh House is to emerge out of previous experiential limitations into a new kind of relating and uncovering of who we are, who we can be, who we are meant to be in partnership, in communion with one we love. There is always that sense of coming into a new habitat, putting behind us what has gotten stuck or fixed in past syndromes.

In order to fulfill the Seventh House, we need a perpetual process of mutual impregnation, to spark and generate a whole new life in each other, over and again. Then we are alive to the destiny that we share and not entangled in tepid assumptions and roles.

Everything about our Seventh House experiences is geared toward cutting loose of who we thought we were and coming into a direct sense of somebody more adventuresome, less afraid and lost. An evolutionary power is at work here too, spurring us forward with a zeal.

The only stable factor whatsoever is our continuing to extend feelings and build relations. A Seventh House bond with another is a growth experience, a powerful arena for change, not something we can fall back on and take for granted. It is a real adventure, not something indolent we can flop into. This is what relationship is all about in the times we are entering.

The possibilities are staggering. We can do so much more when we combine forces with somebody linked to us from another level. In essence, this is where spirit comes to bear in our lives. Even if we don't believe in anything intangible, the Living Spirit will bless us in the Seventh House, most often through a literal one-to-one sharing with somebody who brings us spirit access just by being there in our lives. All folk people instinctively know that love as spirit's domain.

The greatest dilemma we face in a strong ongoing union with another is that we must also deal with ourselves. Only a strong bond will bring up everything we need to see. Throughout many cycles, we come to stand naked and revealed—and so we must yield, bow before the wisdom of the shared organism. We shall not get away from ourselves in this other, not for long.

The most wondrous facet of Seventh House activity is that we are here at our sharpest, clearest, most emphatically mobilized and keenly motivated. Any planet here can be dialogued with, worked through, optimized. We are seeking the fullest expression of that planet in this lifetime.

Our perpetual struggle is to be as present for another as here for ourselves in the Seventh House. This cannot happen if we have already decided against ourselves. Being friend, lover, and companion to oneself is a requirement for making such a relationship with another.

Intimacy is not something that comes flowing into us from the outside. It's how we carve out a true inner space in the sparkling panoply of energies and beings arriving from elsewhere. In order for us to be adept in true association, we must move seamlessly between the flow of the novel other and the familiar substance of ourselves. As the one inside learns to be in tune with the one outside, the Seventh House comes to fruition. Gropings and desperations cease. Each link is time-less, serene, and self-complete.

Aries

To be Aries is to see before your mind's eye a picture of freedom, of open spaces, of moving without hindrance. It is to go for that picture—and it is to eliminate almost everything else along the way.

To do Aries is to test the self, try the self, push the self, pull the self, never let the self be. It is to be after something. It is to keep on push-ing toward what is both elusive and right there.

To get to the core of Aries is to do something rare and difficult, something worth risking the effort. As we go deeper, we at first find that Aries is consciously and aggressively manufacturing a surface self to stand in for the deep self, to be taken by everybody as the real thing. The surface version is straight-on, instantly all there, ready for any-thing. It is a good puppet self to wield. Like everything Aries does, it is an effective version, one guaranteed to please and to do its job.

Deeper down in here, the Aries soul is alive, in constant conversa-tion with the surface personality, talking the outer one through, keep-ing its coordinates clear. Yet the deeper soul does all this with one side of the brain. The other side of awareness is pondering, reflecting, searching, wondering, and even brooding upon mysteries, hidden layers, upon all that is not apparent. Aries will seldom speak for this side—but it is the reflective awareness that captivates the Aries soul far more than any instant-action scenarios.

If we probe further into that reflective space, we will find that Aries is fascinated, enthralled, entirely awe-struck by the unknown, the unexplainable, the X-factor which shows up everywhere and keeps Aries riveted to her seat. There is this ultimate love affair going with the future, the challenging, missing element, whatever cannot be immediately grasped, taken hold of, or that the Aries will cannot make to seem obvious.

This imagination or inner space generates not only a world of delights, but a web of undercurrents with disturbing elements. A big part of the Aries preoccupation inside is with whatever isn't working, whatever jumps out —and is problematical. When the secret soul obsesses upon what is most painful or strange, such X-factors will show up everywhere and become the main spur to Aries volatility.

Even more destructively, Aries is certain that he can do battle with whatever stands in the way or causes a situation to be hard. He challenges the occasion—so his desire to be absorbed in hidden infinities and his outer self of fabulous surface capacities merge. Placing himself in jeopardy, he often lives for the dramas and the complications that follow him around.

Aries is trying to do something that is half brilliantly inspired and half crazed. He is attempting to tackle the outward and inward conflicts and struggles of his immediate world and to mediate these, or at least improve them. Seldom does he recognize what he's actually doing; mostly he dreams it up. Then he finds himself right there with it, asked to do the impossible, thrilled yet apprehensive.

The ultimate task for Aries is to overcome self. The usual track toward that is to vanquish external versions of internal distractions. Doing it this way dissuades Aries from busting himself in the process of busting what he senses as unreal or untrue.

In Aries country, there must be trickery and deception. Everything is far too straight on to begin with. There's gotta be an edge—so self and world become partners in a complex dance where projection is rampant and you can't really tell where any boundary holds. This is wild to live with, yet inescapable. This blurring of all delineations and limits marks the pathway toward free life.

Aries is devoted to, fabulously involved with significant others. Romance, sexuality, and great throes of soul bonding are Arian forces to reckon with and keep freeing up. They move beyond the perpetual temptation to repeat the past, to become engrossed within regressive contexts, and to rationalize every bit of it as just-what-is-happening.

Because the interior reflective consciousness is so omnivorous for meaning and movement forward, the destiny force in Aries' direction tends to be progressive and magically ready for every next phase. The talents and strengths of Aries stunningly, boundlessly evident, its core gift of co-creating optimal realities from the inside emerges as one of the most needed and vitally relevant of qualities any sign can carry.

The character focus for Aries must be to enjoy, to make the most of, to live completely into what is here now. If the here and the now have many rooms to inhabit, so much the better. The sign of sheer attention to what is right in front of us discloses a whole lot here and endows its world with utmost magnitude.

Mercury

Mercury is a wanderer. Travelling extensively, whether physically or mentally, outer or inner, surfacey or deep, Mercury keeps on journeying, lost in its reverie, wakening to a truth, getting new bearings, forgetting everything previously known.

The function of Mercury is to take the many levels we live upon and to juggle them, shift them, seek out novelty and surprise. Because we are too predictable and set, we need a mischief maker who can confound us, mislead us, show us a different way we would never find if we were in an ordinary state of mind.

However, Mercury is ultra-responsive to outer reflection. If a rationalistic world conditions Mercury from adolescence onward, the Mercury wings will be clipped and a very tame version will emanate. Mercury wants to do whatever will work. If we ask him for a tightly reasonable world, he will oblige. If we insist instead upon something a bit more interesting and alive, Mercury will be there, fabricating his interpersonal magic with aplomb, alacrity, the greatest of ease.

Mercury becomes in our times a multi-phase process. First we take on the mainstream culture through the media and live out that fantasy version, the pragmatic aspect, whichever role seems to fit us. This can last quite a while. But gradually, we lose all fresh interest in deceiving ourselves by extroverting so completely. Then we get in on the mystery. We perceive the healing, the mediation of opposites, and other extraordinary dimensions of Mercury. We become a storyteller, a chronicler, someone alive to a new theme and its resonance. We break our world open, and then Mercury dashes into a bright sparkling realm of outlandish possibilities.

Mercury the wanderer really wants us to live on the fringe between regular workaday consciousness and liminal states. He needs to navigate fluidly between and among and not call any state of mind his own. The greatest wandering is to steer from definition, identity, habitual and conventional categories and explanations. The planet most susceptible to getting caught in those flat worlds is most eager to usher us across into worlds he has dreamed up for the occasion.

The voice of Mercury is all voices in one. It is every world we enter, every self we've ever been, each idea and impulse we have toward the future. Mercury is multiple, ever-shifting, originary. In Mercuryland, nothing has been decided yet, and every direction must be consulted, included, honored in the circle of moving from here.

Generally speaking, we have been suppressive of Mercury, suspicious of him, indulgent toward him in other ways. We use him up; we don't respect his style. For Mercury has this one bright idea permeating everything about him. He believes you've got to let go of yourself to find what is real and alive. If we do let go, we become light and witty and changeable. How can anybody depend upon such a character?

Mercury is after something far more thrilling than being sound and reliable. Mercury wants this moment to come completely alive as a focal point for all free spirits to pour through, stream in, get our attention.

The playful, energetic, all-over-the map Mercury spirit, once it gets going, is the most incorrigible and irrepressible of forces. Trickster, coyote, fool, joker, overturner of tradition and semblance, pure Mercury is a visitor from another plane, gracing us by his peculiar grace of not letting us sit in our easy chairs.

The ultimate track of Mercury is to flip us over, turn us inside out, expose our vulnerability to whatever side we previously missed. In fast transitional worlds Mercury is the one we must turn to. A connoisseur of chaos, a maestro of reworking primal soil amidst hectic and manic proliferation of forces, a borderline spy and guide, he knows his way around; he gives spice to our daily existence.

Mercury delights in extremes, bizarre edges, perverse twists—but only because he is the one we need so badly to counter the program we take on and enslave ourselves within. Mercury just notices, points out, can't miss that the President of the United States is anything but a real president.

The Mercury joke is ultimately on us. We deflect Mercury like an infestation of insects only to find ourselves in a bug's life. We pretend so much is trivial, yet the little things trip us up or draw us back to center. We can't overthrow Mercury and still have it our way.

From a cosmic perspective, Mercury is clearing us of our preconceptions and tired routines, in order to allow something vaster to slip in and turn the tide. Mercury is secretly working for the pivot of the circle. When the world is out of orbit, of course it is Mercury who has a plan. Just follow him blindfolded, fingers crossed. At least you'll have fun and a chance to join the circus.

The Eighth Life Stream

The Eighth House

Walking through the Eighth House asks us to leave our expectations and demands at the house cusp, at the door, and to enter upon a process that will take us everywhere we need to go. Our soul journey is coming to its peak expression. All it takes is a naked, direct approach, willing to venture, able to risk, not stopping when the going gets strange and unpredictable.

Our capacity to reckon with our own previous limitations and to renounce their tenacious grip is most decisive here. Past limits become the secondary enactment of the Eighth House. We must engage these with the same passionate abandon we would give to the open journey of the soul toward the future.

In the Eighth House we replay past scenarios from other lifetimes, or from previous cycles in this lifetime, picking up their drama, color, magnetism, compulsive realism. Even though the "becoming" is a reenactment, a repeat performance, we do it anew with great gusto—for we are trying subconsciously to consume the past in this direct experiential way.

Our greatest struggle inside the Eighth House is to emerge through an overwhelming barrage of past secondary impressions into a whole new state of being. The terrible part is that we may indeed have a saboteur in our midst, a self-saboteur who prefers repeat performances and identifies with the karmic circuit as the only real one to which to belong.

The true primal Eighth House experience arises when we no longer hold back in secondary worlds but commit ourselves to a difficult present course of action. Our resolve must be to get on with our destiny, our pathway in this world, and all that it involves. Once we grow accustomed to the pace of evolution brought on by a freer flow of willingness, the true Eighth House ushers us across into that existence we have always sought.

As we meet a sparkling bright world, one permeated with spirit presence and force, our task is to activate that world within the common Earth. To do so, we must voyage beyond who we thought we were and uncoil a selfhood, taking our very greatest strength and riding it homeward.

Each of us is given an Eighth House primary gift, a capacity that can bear us through the considerable challenges of facing up against collective and personal pitfalls. This house is where we make our spiritual reputation—for we will be asked to slay the ghost of all pasts, in order to bring spirit to bear livingly in this world.

If we tap our central strength, we will find ourselves among universal scenarios highlighting the pivotal lessons and issues of our times, including where we live and what everybody here is moving through. We will be watched carefully by the guiding spirits to see how far we are able to penetrate through phenomenal appearances, how well we are able not to fall for momentary traumatic extremes and their undertow.

Linkages with others in the Eighth House are profound, as we pull in deep alliances and formidable cycles with key karmic buddies. In order to fulfill an Eighth House connection we need to merge with another. Where we take this inside counts the most.

The merging with the other leads us toward a full-on linking with the Living Spirit and with the greater destiny we are called to. This course involves extended battles, identity struggles, and most especially, discovering together with another who we can be and who we are *not* meant to be this time around.

The core adventure of the Eighth House, both unto self and in tandem, is to give of self completely to one's path and receive back an empowerment that enables us to move through our world with confidence, strength, and mobility. We can become an evolutionary agent of collective change with deep bodily feeling. Called to take up who we are in ever-greater spirals, we must not allow any impasse to be definitive or something on which to fall back and lose momentum.

In every sense, Eighth House experience is a blessing. Here we can move great distances and activate our soul force. The Eighth House is a future realm; it gives a multiple field of cosmic connections to feel and sense, to become ever more alive within. All we need in order to make this house our own is to dare, to follow vision, to believe in and take off with our inward striving and instincts. For here we are on the way into that place we always dream toward.

Libra

The sign of Libra offers us an exquisite conundrum of wonders and agonies, all mixed together in a destiny paste. This Libra mix is what we consume all the time. The balance between the extremes is elusive, yet something we must find. Otherwise, we are ripped open by extremes at such a fever that we ease off the total destiny experience of Libra and seek coolness and contemplation in its place.

Libra's wonders are magnificent. To be able to touch so many powerful emotional places over and again is a stunning revelry of artistry and lovingness. To be in the crux point, celebrating, rhapsodizing, hailing the moment is Libra's nature. Here we travel through a variety and multiplicity of worlds each and all of which caress us, welcome us, give us what we need as we venture further.

The agonies of Libra are legion. So many things get to us; so much in life runs us through the middle, feels lacerating or devastating. We are plunged into situations we must traverse, but we get caught and sucked under and this sensation is very hard to live with. We even get pulled back into worlds long ago left behind. The Libran agonies are marked by being in the wrong place at the wrong time and sensing that we've got more of this to take on before we break free and become more expansively ourselves again.

The real path of Libra is to take just the right measure of wonders and delights with just the right measure of consuming agonies with their own messages and deep meanings. To live all of it faithfully and to keep growing and evolving sufficiently to tap greater destiny dynamism is the Libra path.

In order to be masterful and crystal clear, Libra must submit to an identity-ordeal of the utmost urgency. There is no sign of the zodiac more confused about selfhood. Are there borders and boundaries? Who is this one inside, and what responsibility do they truly bear for others? Is the separative egoic self at its strongest or weakest in Libra?

The Libra identity-ordeal is to face a void self, an excessively full self, and a vacillation between them. At the same time, this is a complex identity picture that needs to be changed fundamentally. The void self abandons one's center like dropping a hot potato. The excessively full self is vain and narcissistic and immersed within one's own personal field of emotions. Vacillation between these two poles occurs because both of them are distorted, one-sided, and unsatisfactory.

The ordeal itself is to suffer the simultaneous consequences of excessive self-fullness and extreme self-emptiness. The chameleon soul shifts with the wind and is not really here in the middle for more than a flash. Such a predicament is immobilizing, though one which Libra cannot avoid. She finds herself playing out stuck places endlessly.

There is a path beyond endless crossroads; however, even this juncture tends to be shadowed by having created such substantive worlds in both directions—too much self and too little—that it will shake up everybody around Libra. And that is only if the Libran at long last gets it that being all things to all people is a losing game in a deeper, ultimate reckoning.

Up to this point in the journey, Libra puffed up with self where this was called for and got rid of self where that seemed to be the indication. The greater Libra journey keys on following solely internal cues for identity. For Libra this is a huge, Earth-shattering repolarization.

When the inside is respected, a revolution follows in all aspects of life. Most powerfully, the deeper soul regions are at long last given their due. To feel one's inward feelings and embody one's deeper emotions allows a Libran to live inside their body in a full sense. And then the Libra story comes true.

Before, there were intimations of this stage, brief flare-ups in anticipatory form. To live from within for Libra is a possibility not just to be imagined but to be embraced as a constant. Otherwise, it doesn't happen. This is to be genuine with the same fluency and attunement as one previously merely attained while acting out. Then spirit becomes an actual pulsating force right here, accompanying every breath, bringing blessings and grace, not vanishing like a chimera with each next upheaval.

A vast destiny awaits Libra, though it often has to be suspended a long time. When readiness is there, the fruits are abundant. The entire Libra journey has been teaching in secret ways everything one needs to know about the Earth Curriculum. Now these deeper gleanings become wakeful and shareable.

Libra has been immersed within the shadow lesson of what not to do, strategies which play into the hands of conditioning and controlling forces. In the ripeness of time, Libra can embrace the light and stay true, without feeling her truth to be unstable or subject to doubt. To believe in self serenely and to honor the whole of one's life with a full heart is the consummate destination for Libra. Then her stark surreal journey becomes a gem, and those struggles with self allow her to feel for everybody here.

Mars

We demand of ourselves that we use Mars as often as possible. We are living in a world where we must lean on our Mars over and over again. This quantitative Mars prevails in the collective karmic mix, where it is unconscious, automatic, impulsive, driven, chaotic, and immensely effective.

We use the quantitative Mars like a weapon or blunt instrument to achieve our goals and enforce our intention. It becomes muscle and emphasis—an exclamation point. We call upon Mars to back us up, to shift fast into fourth gear, to turn us into well-oiled machines. We know we need to be visible, a tangible factor—and Mars will get us there.

It is easy for us to identify this as masculine and warrior-like—but the quantitative Mars has become something of a technological wonder nowadays. We are mass-producing Mars everywhere on Earth to make outer material existence viable, potent, and inescapable. Mars is the enforcer of the code of "more is better."

Though we are exploiting Mars to the hilt, this quantitative Mars is an imposter. He has nothing to do with the qualitative Mars, or with, shall we say, the real blood-and-guts Mars. So let us drop the outer version and gaze upon the hidden Mars, the one that substantively matters.

The deeper core Mars is devoted to pulling us into those spaces that challenge us to extend our range of self-expression. The outer situation becomes one which we cannot sleepwalk through any longer or negotiate by mere habit. The real Mars wants us to show up here. To do so requires us to overcome everything in us that is afraid of Mars, that is disconnected, that doesn't care, that won't do it.

Mars is the champion of radical self-overcoming. He is convinced that we have something out ahead of us to become. He is certain that in order to get there, we will be forced by all factors to confront and clear everything in us that has become old and used up. He is ardent and willing to do whatever it takes to draw us right through the middle of the obstacles we face along this destiny journey.

Mars' shadow is that his relentless, ruthless, and forward-propelling instincts and emotions are not yet synchronized with the whole of our being and so he tends to dominate us and push his will upon us, upon the more sensitized facets of self and world. This imposition of ferocious emotional intensity and drive can easily become almost as dark and heavy as Mars traditionally was reputed to be.

For ultimate Mars to get straight requires that our penetration through Earthly density navigate the personal quantum of it that we can assimilate. Some of us need to be primal, direct, and forceful in our way of being in this world. For others this violent external thrust is neither healthful nor steady. Heavy-handed Mars is far more option-al than he knows.

Interpersonally, Mars leads to lots of complications. If one person is Mars plus and the other Mars minus—as is often the case—dread conflicts arise. Where Mars goes, conflicts of interest necessarily follow. How much of that fiery energy do we want still to play out between us? Even more to the point, what is optimal in the greater picture for the future?

Here we come upon a great surprise. Contrary to many current left-ist ideologies, Mars is super-key to our common future. He's not going to get weaker. Instead, he will come on stronger than ever, but in a transmuted form.

The purpose of Mars in the near future is to awaken us out of the collective lethargy of the nineteenth and twentieth centuries, to engage us passionately and internally mobilize us into a way of life previous cycles did not allow. Mars is onto something big nowadays. He sees a spurting forward into previously unoccupied space, and this fires him into renewed determination to voice an alternative, a way forward, a path beyond.

We have become consciousness-propelled and life-force-sloppy. We tend to promote clever intelligence, discounting the organismic impulse toward new life. In order to allow Mars his voice in our future, to empower Mars rightfully, we must clear out the clutter of mind's end-less hiding places.

Our own vital Mars is a portal into the unknown, a doorway into the unfamilar and uncomfortable places inside us. He is youthful always, fresh and devoid of inhibitions. He thrives on guts and self-possessed presence. He is as audacious and irrepressible as we can let him be.

Mars can also turn into a peacemaker, a selfless upholder of the sacred, a spokesperson for progressive vision and idealism. As his innermost voice calls him to embody what we have forgotten and denied, Mars seeks a world where all of us are mutually empowering and enhancing. Placing our personal will on the altar of the universal good is the ultimate domain of future Mars. If he can puncture his own illusions and stay on track with where we are going together, he will become a mouthpiece for our indispensable truths and shared realizations.

The Ninth Life Stream

The Ninth House

The total realm of the Ninth House will enact itself, regardless of whether it is seen outwardly, interpreted falsely, or internally denied. It exists unto itself and creates its own reality in every plane of existence. We can look away or we can gaze straight upon it as it happens here.

As we have seen in the previous house, the core self wishes to bring up before itself each and every facet that has blocked the greater path and kept the karmic wheel spinning. This project then becomes the central cornerstone of the Ninth House operation, empowering lost self-fragments to do more than they have done in previous houses. The core self specifically intends them to reveal their fatal flaw, to repeat their pivotal lessons, and to do all of this while knowing better. Skillfully enacted, the Ninth House is effective and straight. Ordinarily, we don't do things that way.

Other layers of self typically will become fascinated with what is happening here, swathed up within a complex of self-absorption. A rapt audience witnesses karmic replays and recapitulations with a different kind of attention than the core self is generating. Consequently, our soul hunger and thirst for viewing self and world and others enacting this ritual-drama can become addictive to the point of insatiable.

The key to Ninth House awakening then becomes to see through one's own self-fascination in every variation of grandiosity, inflation, self-importance, self-magnifying. To see self larger than life and be caught in the witness of it is a corrupting position, one that must be countered by spiritual discipline, by dedication to the core self. All secondary layers of personal soul engulfment within the mirage must be dispersed.

Meanwhile, the core self remains inwardly gazing upon all that is unfolding—a contemplative stillness that is always there. Not impressed by any of it, nor sitting in dark judgment of it, the core self merely has this need to view it all passing, free it, and open the space it occupies. The detachment and clarity of the core self in the midst of such madness is remarkable.

In a decadent civilization at the end of its tether, this least collective of all houses becomes an entrenched minority of one. There tends to arise a separative sphere, surrounded by a moat. The interior is kept deep inside. The exterior is met in formal, strict terms. Inside of this pattern can develop a host of excesses, all in the direction of being captivated by one's own specialness, uniqueness, and destiny magnitude.

Each and every way we get lost in the Ninth House is a reflection of the same syndrome. We get hooked on identifying ourselves with familiar, fixed layers of selfhood that are controlling, powerful, and overly respected by others. We buy into our own images, our pictures. We invent ourselves to be as we dread, as we hope, as we fear, as we assume.

The true Ninth House is the overcoming of all of these limitation scenarios, even the most magnificent of them. In their place we construct an open and cosmically responsive space. We no longer tell ourselves anything about who we once were or who we must be. Instead, we make room for our core self to show us a different way, in alignment with greater cosmic powers.

We also make sure to keep emptying and opening. We allow a true witness to see through our eyes and feel through our body. We make ourselves available for spirit to source our situation, our ongoing life commitment. We don't need to know, don't have to be together or on top of everything that arises. Anyone who acts as if they are in charge here is just following a slavish old script.

Now we refuse to impose preconceived ideas, superstructures onto any living being, starting with ourselves. We work to keep clearing away sociocultural clutter. Instead of making ourselves into somebody, we ask what is intended here.

The Ninth House eventually becomes the place where we give our most essential being its chance to express and embody a non-violating, non-ideological vision. We revel in the chance to quicken the deeper, higher places and integrate them by our own intuiton.

The task of the Ninth House is to recreate self to be what it truly is. Those working here true to purpose at every juncture manifest a wild kind of self-acceptance and life-embrace that just keeps on getting more irrepressibly free.

Capricorn

It is impossible for Capricorn to know something and then not build a life around demonstrating it. But does Capricorn know self? Does Capricorn know the one inside? Or is Capricorn mesmerized by the outward image of the one who performs, who demonstrates, who makes the invisible tangible and palpable?

Capricorn is a spiral vortex action, spinning on an inward axis ever closer to the center. Capricorn is pure process, but pervasively tyrannized by the image of needing to arrive at the finish line, or else be considered a failure. Yet Capricorn must take on more than can be fulfilled. By definition Capricorn is going to fall short of her mark.

Psychological matters tend then to dominate the Capricorn soul realm. Traditionally, these were karmic substantive matters of character and endurance, suffering and ultimate redemption. But now Capricorn stands before consciousness that knows its own limitations and flaws. Truth to tell, it is an awesome task for Capricorn to say yes to the inner self on any terms that are real.

Capricorn involves: What do we do with the No? How can we come to terms with the endless tragedy and heartache of life? Can we know these things while still remaining affirmative, celebrational, and in touch with wholeness? Will we indulge ourselves shamelessly in domains everybody now knows are purely destructive? Can the shame and the guilt, the shadow and the old stuff be cut through with sufficient conviction and power that we will remain on the side of the gods and not twist perversely against and against and against?

The solitary, lonely, rugged path for Capricorn is to heal, to forgive, to renounce all righteousness, most especially that righteousness directed against self. Capricorn's impossibly steep trajectory in our times is to make up for a backlog of generations and lifetimes of self against self, self against life, and life against self. Capricorn inherits from past selves, from early life, from ancestors a formidable, harsh, grim scenario of self-estrangement, of tooth and claw. Can Capricorn come back in touch indeed?

Such a quest can only succeed in an authentic spiritual dimension, now as ever. Meaning is vital for Capricorn. Value is everything. Spirit is the source of all true meaning and value. The most skeptical of signs, the one most plagued by doubt, the one most susceptible to nihilisms and pragmatic materialisms needs a sacred understanding of life to get through the knots of shadow.

The testing action for Capricorn is to keep the self away from spirit at the moment it most craves spirit, to cut the self off from whatever is most desired. Coming through this test is to cast off the oppression of a proud layer of selfhood that in fact keeps taking on these trials blindly. Getting through Capricorn's pride and stubbornness is a mighty ordeal.

Capricorn is simply attached to false selves, identified with what enslaves and postpones the inevitable. Capricorn has a hard time weaning itself from the habit of going for the dark semblance and missing the bright core. An intoxication with being wrong, being damned, being stopped by this-and-that force is the snare for Capricorn. Yet there is a way past all of these shadows. There is indeed a clear pathway up the mountain and through the mountain.

The essential path of Capricorn is to raise the self to the next higher frequency and from that place to free it of what was previously nagging, while developing a tough compassion for the one who takes on the lies. A double action must be there to burst Capricorn free. The expanding awareness has to be as ruthlessly lucid as Capricorn craves; yet the soul conscience needs to be willing to acknowledge the necessity and reality of each and every limiting pattern as well as one's relation to it all along the way.

If the space of the greater self is cleared ahead and the lesser self is honored and valued on its own terms, Capricorn will build up no fresh karma. As soon as nothing is scorned or despised, the bulk of Capricornian shadows dissolve.

The temptation to see something scathingly wrong and hold it in sights that way is simply the thickest shadow a sign could attract. Nobody can grapple with that kind of baggage any longer. We must slay the perfectionist if we are to have any chance.

A brutally intense life lesson dominates Capricorn's development. Do not elevate anything at anything else's expense. Do not put anybody down in order to raise somebody else up. Realize that all sides are working for the same boss and are taking on their roles with a wink and a nod.

The true Capricorn emerges—simply a woman or man of utmost integrity, from top to bottom. He witnesses all that he does and corrects it in the light of spirit wisdom. She takes herself lightly. For she realizes that her part is to dance with destiny. And to dance that dance enduringly, you must get out of your own way and let the light shine through as it will.

Uranus

None of us can do without Uranus. Uranus orchestrates our remarkable comeback from being counted out personally, individually, collectively, globally.

Uranus sizes up our barrier against becoming who we are—and then designs a master plan, one brilliant enough to outwit all internal adversaries. This must be done from a place that is free of exterior restraints. So we don't know, except in rare flashes, what Uranus is up to. That way, however, the greater strategy can prevail in the end.

The core principle behind each and every one of the Uranian maneuvers is the paradoxical understanding that we don't wish to be exposed and we need to be exposed and both of these are true in the same place at the same time. The skillful means is to expose a facet of self that we can surrender, while protecting the rest of self against premature exposure.

Uranus is the one inside, behind the scenes, perfectly in accord with all guiding powers and all greater intelligences. The manifestation of Uranus in our lives is dazzlingly deceptive. Every once in a great while we see in a Uranian way, and the rest of the time we don't know Uranus at all. But reality must be entirely and steadily founded upon Uranus and its vaster consciousness stream, with knowing how to keep the little ego-mind happy with ways it maintains outer control. It is strictly the wise one inside who oversees what we are doing while choosing to remain incognito.

If we plunge to the inside of Uranus and leave behind its outer politics, we come upon a sparkling jewel of direct undiluted perception of self, of world, of each and every decisive factor. This perception is lit up from within by the presence of our ultimate truth, just behind the scenes of Uranus. In essence, Uranus masks boundless truth by taking up one strand of it and specializing in it super-intensively.

In most instances, our optimal Uranian superconscious awareness is directed toward eliminating lies and deceptions and, whatever this involves, getting to a true place. Usually, Uranus targets some especially opaque area of self-blindness, hammering away at it with every conceivable means. Fortunately, it chooses us; we don't have to set it going.

Why would we need such a relentless approach from such a high source to counter our personal ways of obstructing destiny? Because in recent centuries we have become experts at stopping ourselves cold. When Uranus was discovered outwardly in 1781, we had to enlist a cosmic advocate to take our part against false voices within and without.

Swept up in a momentum of pursuing and tracking down each and every place we are tuned out of, we tap all available resources. It is vital that each of us realize that this is happening. Without Uranus at work, we would be where our mind tells us we are—and if Uranus were not so adroit at concealing itself, we would have stopped it long ago.

Uranus is the wizard within—the great subtle magician of our lives. There are a few among us who let Uranus all the way through.

With single-minded intent, an unimpeded Uranus will align our every action and thought with the greater design for our lives. It will calibrate, integrate, make coherent, and steady the form and spirit levels through multiple interplay. Uranus seeks to make it clear that the most ultimate and the most basic facets of awareness are feeding into the same source, coming from the same place, doing the same exact thing.

If we follow Uranus with conviction and selfless willingness, we find our lives reversed. Instead of believing that everything is working against us, we keep discovering empirically that *all* factors are there to liberate us.

The Uranian sword of awakening is an awesome spectacle. We keep seeing and feeling the precise one we remember we are; we become who we always sought to become. The veils fall away; the truth becomes so inescapable we can't manufacture the slightest melodrama to put off self-recognition.

When we have enlisted Uranus to counter our multiple madness with singular wisdom throughout modern times, we knew what we were doing. We sent out a cosmic call for all the galactic realms to come back into view and play their part, toward a cosmic age ahead. Now that age is fast approaching. We have found a gateway to the outer planets unknown to the ancients, and Uranus continues to serve us well and deserves the vastest gratitude.

The Tenth Life Stream

The Tenth House

At the opening or cusp of the Tenth House, we are ushered through a portal, traditionally known as the Midheaven, yet more truly described as the Heavenly Crown. The Crown Signature on the cusp aligns us with worlds beyond this particular time frame. The planets we place within the Tenth House ensoul our greater-worlds alignment by calling us to fulfill a task or mission, take on a destiny, become a world, represent Heaven in Earth.

Along our way toward uncovering what we are meant to do here in this lifetime, our Crown nature puts us through a sequence of changes which define our very existence. Most of these center around casting off very persistent, tough patterns and syndromes we have taken on in place of our greater life task. Just the process of moving through these ultra-significant blocks and barriers often detains us.

We feel then, in the midst of our destiny crisis, often as though we cannot get there from here. What will it take for us to dismantle structures that are this formidable? Well, it will take either a cracking open of the Crown itself to admit the light of the greater worlds directly, or a microcosmic reflection of the same dynamic, by coming to a place inside ourselves where what we had assumed and even championed previously becomes no longer appealing and we know we are intended to be somebody else altogether. This change of heart is vital and may repeat itself a few times. For we are carrying much baggage and it is time to dump it all, in the cycles given for this.

As we rise through the layers of our previous ideas and values, we keep coming into a more open world. In the Tenth House, we often emerge from closed ancestral and collective systems. In our perseverance to overthrow what is too tight a fit, we stumble upon a greater life altogether. This revelation implicitly requires us to express and to embody what we are realizing so that others can also find their way to these extraordinary places. We are all heading there anyway.

The thrust of intention, of longing, of need to be whole and complete is very strong and powerful in the Tenth House. We know we must optimize our capacities this time around. There is no further place to hide. We have risen to the top of the world, and everybody is watching what we do.

Although we are playing quite dramatic roles upon the world stage, we must develop a knack of not getting inwardly impressed by how everybody around us sees us, at least in an outer context. This skill is well worth cultivating. Its crucial lesson is to be spacious and dispassionate in how we witness our own expression in the world, while still emphasizing deep commitment and involvement with what is needed here.

The harsh dilemma of the Tenth House is its assignation with shadow phenomena—neglected and forsaken, denied and suppressed components of self and world. To be able to honor the dark side—to embrace intelligently darkness and lingering shadows while rallying others toward the bright side—places a special burden on this House. We are meant to be encompassing, universal, inclusive in our grasp of the world through the Crown—but we tend to move toward light, ideals, hopes, and dreams.

Many of us will eventually devote our entire Tenth House attunement to a life work, a set of tasks which serves our larger community and allows our family and friends to be an integral part of the whole. Quite often, this vocational drive will fashion us and forge us into an instrument for greater purposes to be enacted, even though our own outer awareness is not able to sustain a specific sense of how this is operating.

The Tenth House is meant to be a conduit for spirit to speak, to work its truth into every fiber of life. Yet the most resonant spirit is often not outwardly packaged in spirit form; it can exist in a fashion that is quite subtle and personal and apparently commonsensical. What matters is its integrity. As we allow our highest wisdom and greatest truth sensibility to permeate our lives and our work in the world, we are doing spirit's business.

There lives upon the Crown as well a vaster capacity, to which we can become awake as we ripen and mature. Generously and compassionately we let ourselves become a true teacher, a real way-shower. If we persist in assimilating life's lessons through the Tenth House, such a stage is natural and inevitable.

This ultimate dimension of the Heavenly Crown is there from the beginning. We are raised to our highest frequency and guided, inspired, instrumented to make this frequency one through which others can tap us. Then exquisite fruition is at hand. We are setting the tone for tomorrow's world by becoming transparent to Universal Spirit—the suprapersonal conduit that is most needed in this world at this time—bearing a fluent immediacy that touches every soul.

Cancer

The sign of Cancer is the hardest one to understand. It is especially difficult for Cancerians to grasp their own sign. Let us take a journey to find out why this energy frequency is so elusive, so easily missed.

As a strategy develops of hiding out in one's own opposite polarity, Cancer becomes shadow, makes its own generic statement, and gravitates toward innocuous and undemanding style and substance. But all of this is simply to protect a massive vulnerability and to enclose the self within a chamber that can allow growth and development away from prying eyes.

These things are often necessary because the real Cancer is at one with her world—a dangerously abusable position. If Cancer is not careful, all of those closest to her will turn her into the universal caregiver, the perfect mother, the ideal housewife, the businessman who is sober and responsible and ethical and makes it all work for everybody. The one way she can instinctively throw off the avalanche of roles and demands is by pretending to be dumb, simple, unremark-able, someone nobody would turn to for important things.

Thus, we have two Cancers—the overt one and the covert one. The overt Cancer is momentarily cast and recast in whatever forms are most basic, acceptable, and easy to take on and take off. Even though extended cycles may be spent frozen inside of a particular overt Cancerian mask, the covert Cancer is always plotting her escape and forever dis-identifying with the present version taken on. The overt Cancer is a dissociated prototype, alienated and depersonalized. The covert Cancer is as intriguing and profound as the overt Cancer is conventional and mass-oriented. So let us speak no more of the sur-faces and dive into the soul of Cancer, the deep underbelly, the high Cancerian overtone.

Cancer exists within a matrix, a formative design which is tailor-made for her. Invisible worlds are her friends and intimates. Cancer is a child of inner worlds, core worlds, the bridge from them into outer domains.

Yet there are many under places and points of enchantment or sus-pension, as the sign of Cancer is greatly susceptible to carrying around barnacles and burdens of worlds gone wrong, of karmas that haunt, of secret allegiances that are still not being integrated successfully. Cancer exists in a void or vacuum where such negative factors take charge. It is stunning how often this occurs. Then Cancer doesn't know herself, can't circulate freely. She is caught in a trap sprung to keep her back from what she is here for.

Cancerians can tap vital resources and secret source-springs; they retain great intrinsic power to change their habitual pattern. All they have to do is be willing to admit what has happened and that they need true guidance. The path of Cancer is keyed into these turn-arounds. One extreme cycle, once the lesson is taken hold of, begets an entirely different phase. Cancer is excellent at learning core les-sons, even if it takes a thousand years.

The story of Cancer is that of the soul clamoring to fulfill a deep-er purpose and to penetrate through the layers of personal and collective entrapment. This tale is seldom told. We have smothered this level in our times—so it becomes a secret, masked by outer semblances, kept to the self perhaps. This is not acceptable. Everything Cancer moves through is intended for the liberation of all those who need to know what she is coming to realize.

The pivotal overcoming along the Cancerian path is to take the hyper-vulnerable, frightened, and invaded child core of Cancer and to be no longer at the mercy of her phobias and stark introversions. If Cancer can leave her nostalgias and emotional hooks behind, so much energy is freed up, such a great consciousness restored.

Cancer can be a soul-remembrance catalyst. It is given to Cancer to recall, to bear intact the ancient, the timeless, the officially denied aspects of existence. She makes sure that we tap what has been before to guide us as we face the vast unknown ahead.

It is the true gift of Cancer to be in tune with soul timing, grace timing, time beyond time. She is at her best when she shows the way forward while keeping our past and present in her view. It is her task to make futures possible, to make what happens real.

In the largest view, Cancerians are the lineage holders for all invaluable components to be preserved, loved, and revived. This is the true heritage of future children, Cancer spanning generations. She seeds essential qualities passed from life wisdom into life experiment. If she can free herself of the ghosts that bind, Cancer will act as the touchstone of our common future.

Ceres

Each of the four main asteroids (as we have seen) is harboring a twisted faculty that holds behind it something magnificent and really stunning, which the asteroid simultaneously betrays and protects. Ceres is the central asteroid of the four. It is the one we must turn around as the pivot for repolarizing asteroidal consciousness from the trapped form to which we are accustomed into a liberated mode of awareness.

The faculty Ceres is harboring is that of spirit-knowing. We once could, prior to the nineteenth century, access direct spirit-knowing as a given. However, needing to grow up and become independent of the Starry Heavens and their great gods and goddesses, we detoured around our still-remaining spirit-knowing and distracted ourselves by developing many outer Ceres gifts, things that would look and seem to be just as good as, if not far better than, what we'd lost in the process. Look at every Search for Extraterrestrial Intelligence.

The twisted version of Ceres turns everything into our own opinion, our own special outlook, our private life philosophy and ideological position. We have become personal-values evaluators, judges, controllers. In the midst of doing so, we have gone off on a tangent into the strangest byways of the mind.

Ceres adopts a model, a prototype. It emulates a culturally popular or sophisticated version of what is most admirable and impressive. Then it swallows itself up in the procedures needed to operate that way. She wants to be influential and important. Yet every bit of this is soaked up in an outer sense—one big elaborate manipulation of image and impression.

In the asteroidal terms of the nineteenth and twentieth Centuries, we have come to believe, to the most elaborate extents, in the power of public self-presentation. We are so blindly magnetized by the celebrities and experts that we imagine that such personae are somehow real and true. This is the Ceres trance. We each try to become some kind of special person for others to flatter and praise.

What we least tune into are the feet of clay which accompany every single Ceres presentation. An outer fame resonates upon an inner emptiness. That emptiness is saturated with undercurrents and forces which sabotage and make miserable what is outwardly so smooth and flawless. This kind of thing proliferates into a madness of gaps and missing parts.

Yet we are now at the precipice of a different world entirely. Our proud self-images, our inflated positions in the world are fragile and precarious. The world beyond the outer mind and its cleverness is coming on strong, and all of us can feel it.

What will a positive Ceres come to, in terms of the spirit-knowing faculty? We are about to restore our greater spirit-knowing; yet it will be far different from the automatic version of Medieval times. Each one of us will need to find within ourselves a true universal taproot with which to be aligned. We will need to keep bringing this taproot to individual expression, in synchronization with stuff that is moving through our entire world. Yet there is a considerable initiation to pass through in order to move out of all betraying popularizations and easy mythologizings of our own mental consciousness. We are drawn to imagine an eternal return to the Medieval, but these are guises and masks, and were never true in the Middle Ages either, except as we made them our collective projection. The leap into true spirit-knowing, without mythological costuming, bites into our deepest soul.

When we became enraptured with public image and the outer mental version of spirit truth, we developed a thick skin of secret skepticism and bone-deep doubt that anything real exists at all in a world where it is so easy to fool people. After all atoms are nothing, time is nonexistent, bodies made of atoms are nothing, or mere numerical rebuses. For the duration of Communism in the Soviet Union and China, billions were not only told but ordered to believe that this life is the whole thing, followed by oblivion. Abnegation of spirit *was* the religion. Don't believe for a moment that the same ideology hasn't permeated the West. We are commanded, albeit more persuasively and hedonistically, to turn everything into material and commodity. Now this thick skin won't let us get back in touch with our greater spirit-knowing, to live from there. Instead, it challenges all movement toward becoming one with the greater worlds (by arguing that such worlds are illusions) and postpones any decisive forays thence as long as possible.

The pragmatic model Ceres has adapted is energetically and vibrationally allergic to the feeling tone of deep, high truth. It goes instead for the consumer version, the popular consumption style, which eliminates any need to work at returning to the heights. This presents quite a hurdle to rehabilitating the pristine wonder of the spirit way. And it is not just a matter of knowing; we must experience it intimately and in a form we can use in every facet of our lives. Then the spirits really will be at hand.

Nonetheless, Ceres is leading the way beyond its own snares. It always was intent on doing so. Now is the time the evolutionary signal is given. Ceres tends to lead us now into a multi-stage initiation of recovering soul from where personality has the one monopoly in town.

The pivotal difference between the outwardly contrived version and the inwardly trained version is that the outer one always has all the answers, either explicitly or implicitly, while the inner one has only questions, probes, open areas to receive and respond to a greater truth consciousness. We were convinced à la the asteroid belt that we were in charge here, we human brains. We are discovering through the metamorphosed asteroid belt that we are in co-creative partnership with all other realms of being and that we serve best when we steer clear of arrogant assumptions.

The Eleventh Life Stream

The Eleventh House

We are granted an opening inside the Eleventh House. In order to respond to the invitation, we will need to stretch and expand all structures, forms, roles, concepts to make room for all that can come into being. This process is quite natural and straightforward. As we let ourselves go into the vaster picture, we can evolve into just about any and every direction and dimension we can conceive of or let into our lives.

An instinct takes over here—the instinct to evolve, the instinct to move far and freely with destiny. When we activate this instinct, we can move forward without being hindered by complications and cross-currents. The evolving instinct generates clearance ahead, a free windy corridor to send us wherever we need to go.

We will also find company upon this extended journey. As we do so, it will bring with it a kind of connection which has very little to do with what we usually think of as what allows people to feel in love. This way of linking, inside the Eleventh House, is much more open-ended, more foundationally free from the beginning. We are seeking to venture with somebody else, rather than to settle into any kind of pattern. Certainly this can become the kind of link where we really know each other, we see and sense and feel the expanding greater self and spark at a level of cosmic quickening.

When we steer our Eleventh House experiences into a more personal framework, they lose their vital edge. Probes into the unknown, they can't be reduced to everyday terms. We need to develop a different vocabulary, a quieter and more deeply tuned in way to grapple with what we draw to ourselves and where it brings us.

The great challenge inside the Eleventh House is to light up, to keep lighting up, and to affirm with real conviction the self within us who can live at an expanded frequency in a comfortable and lively fashion. That part of our being needs to sense what is possible in this world and to make way for it, with a sense of critical urgency. If we surrender, the rest of us can come. If we don't, the cross-currents will take charge. Then we will find ourselves caught in the middle between the most adventuresome reaches of our being and the part of us that can't yet go there and stay.

When we are not quite ready to live our dreams and visions, the Eleventh House becomes our vacation paradise, our release into the blue. We let ourselves be our whole self only under optimal conditions, the rest of the time reverting to prior patterns. Over an extended cycle we get many previews of what it is like to move with the currents of radical change, and we may eventually realize their fulcral power.

Souls who pass through the Eleventh House are often ready for some of the brighter sparks of Earth's incarnation domain. A universal feeling for the connectedness with all of life starts the ball rolling through a world of deep, junglelike texture. Linking with exotic guides and infinite realities gets us in there. Then, if that weren't enough to wow us, great awakening experiences begin.

All of these center around coming to ourselves in a way different from before. An egoistic experience of the Eleventh House makes it seem as though we are personally hugely important and special to be able to stretch out into brighter vistas. But as we make ourselves at home inside the Eleventh House realms, we keep finding that who we are is an entirely different kind of being than who we had been reflected to be previously. The specialness is still thrilling, but also ordinary.

We encounter a future self, a selfless one, who is here truly for everybody, the one we all are looking to become. This vital-essence being emits a radiant field of blessing, grace, and well-being, spreading the richest of energies wherever he goeth.

That brighter self is co-creative, collaborative. It makes real connections everywhere, awaking textures of landscape and relationship. An encouraging and revitalizing energy and awareness meets him when he comes around. Just to be in such a field shifts the pattern for any who allow it.

A presentiment of such an occasion and radiance permeates our Eleventh House experiences. We are moving toward being actively able to advance evolution, to contribute something to where we all are going. This is one of the most full-on energies in the world, seeking restlessly to be expressed, harnessed, and embodied.

While being exposed to such an unlimited potential is a big step for anybody, actually moving in the direction of fulfilling one's cosmic mission is the greatest of leaps. When the times break free and the energies become more directly on tap, Eleventh House improbabilities and impossibilities turn out so basic and ordinary that we can't even remember why they seemed so far out.

Gemini

Something bright arises in Gemini. This brightness wants so badly to come into its own. It seeks to dispel darkness, to neutralize Earthbound difficulties, to make a space for all bright and beautiful things to hold sway. Gemini brightness nurtures ideals and visions, infinite possibilities, and the most amazing scope. All of us root for Gemini to be able to sustain its action and move further.

Something dark and strange worms in from below in Gemini. This suspicion, this doubt and restless wind of wandering far away comes with a macabre energy. Inside the atmosphere of the dark one, everything seems to be so very unlikely, so alienating, so truly absurd. Under that banner people appear driven by vanity and folly, and all you can expect in this world is to be disappointed, to find your worst fears coming true, to crash ineffectually against what felt initially so expansive, so boundless, so free.

The journey of Gemini is to come unto the brightness, to move into a place where duality is no longer at work. To get there requires more than the wits and ingenuity that Gemini brings to every task; it asks for a change of heart, a foundational shift. Only a deep soul-level metamorphosis will bear Gemini through the alternating frequencies of such a great yes and such a dreadful no.

The steps toward making a quantum leap into a whole new life are each one geared toward cutting loose a specific layer of outer mind. Each time, worldly appearances are supportive of the way outer mind believes the situation to be. The Gemini test is to stand in the face of the evidence, the proof, the phenomena, and to penetrate deeper into what is really going on here and what it means.

The claustrophobic part is that Gemini always already knows all the pieces that are being sought. Nothing is really that new or surprising. Yet in the gut check of Gemini reality, the paradoxical relationship between what Gemini knows and does not know is too distorting to be taken seriously to heart. Gemini is familiar with every world he or she can ever find—but to be freshly, fully there in a surrendered and mind-free fashion is a whole different dimension of life from merely entertaining strange notions.

It is a foregone conclusion that at any stage of the journey, Gemini can talk anybody into, and even talk oneself into, whatever version of what is happening seems either appealing or needed. It is exceedingly demanding for Gemini to align with whole soul and body in the spaces invoked by the marvelous powers of consciousness.

When Gemini does move through the duality-bonds of the outer mind and comes into a whole seeing, a very different kind of Gemini emerges from what is either stereotyped or assumed. The very first characteristic will be a true generosity of spirit which, no longer shadowed by critical put-downs, can be free and clear to do its real magic in this world. Generous spirit senses in each creature his or her luminous essence. The true Gemini impulse is to accompany everyone upon the journey of discovering how to be with that sparkling sense of being.

Even the sprung Gemini bears many loose and lazy characteristics, but these count for little. What matters is the spark in their eyes, the recognition in their touch, the all-pervasive body language of knowing *we can do it*. When that feeling tone comes around, it shifts the balance in a major way. People become lighter and far less burdened. They get in tune with their purpose, their bottomless capacity, in a natural way. Marvelous things become self-evident.

Throughout modern times we have been hardput to believe in a truly free Gemini. We love her innocence, her wonder, her promise, her ease. But we have not stood together with Gemini in the direction of co-creating a more vibrantly authentic world. We expect Gemini to fall. We assume that Gemini is only briefly up there, too unearthly to get away with being so bright and weightless beyond its allotted moment of grace.

The hardiest, most incorrigible of signs is Gemini. Moving through inevitable rounds of defeats and frustrations is no big deal in Gemini-Land. Cosmic spark can't land here in any simple, casual way. Tests and trials are inevitable. What's of interest is whether a given strongly Gemini soul can cleave to an innate power of belief and faith and trust, and extend these far enough to slay the old gods of reason.

The ultimate Gemini state is one of moving beyond what has previously proven possible into uncharted waters. Therefore, Gemini is a sign perfectly calibrated to changes of the twenty-first century. It is a sign likely to come into its own in the years ahead.

Always, Gemini has been the seed-bearer for future states of evolution. What has been hard is to wait, to hold steady in harsh times. What has gotten Gemini through is this wild will that cannot sit still for smug and complacent worlds, that cannot stand to tame and condition the boundless soul.

It is the Gemini genius to see through opacity, to sense a further horizon, to link up with totality and root in that place. Gemini is working on becoming present to herself and to others in a more simple, direct, and quiet fashion. She is just learning to be in heart resonance with the striving, struggling one in us all.

The Sun

We live by the Sun inside. Because of our own internal Sun, we belong here in this expanding world. We tap the Sun to tune us into the New Life Wave and to show us where we are meant to go, who we are meant to be.

The Sun is the doorway to all cosmic worlds. If we find sufficient solar warmth and light in our hearts, we can go anywhere, become anything, and still be recognizably ourselves under all circumstances. The Sun is our central flame of identity, our individual selfhood in its essence-manifestation in this world at this time.

Because the Earth stands under the Sun directly opposite, most of us have a very geocentric, an Earth-saturated feeling for the Sun. We caution ourselves not to get sunstroke, not to stare into the sun, not to buy its celestial program. We assume that the Sun is too much for us and that we need to defend ourselves against the inflation that comes with soaking in too much Sun and too little of the more somber and starkly focused energies of the other planets, such as Saturn, the Moon, the Earth herself, and facets of Mercury and Mars.

In many ways, all of this is fair. Few of us are ready to go solar in a more expanded and extended sense. There are strong taboos—tribal, cultural, historical—which show us that our bodies are Earthly, our emotions lunar, and our Sun barrierless with little respect for personae and roles. The Sun is meant to be too much. Or so it would seem.

We are now in an era which features our galaxy expanding, our Earth awakening, our star friends attending from their various orientations, and our human nature in its traditional form no longer sufficient to meet the times.

In the current mix, the future opening power of the Sun, the self-stretching pull of it is both welcome and needed. We are getting pulled towards solar pathways as never before. This serves to make many things possible that would otherwise seem far out of reach.

Most relevantly, the Sun calls us to enter upon a global citizenship, a cutting across lines that have held people unto themselves. The Sun is universally pounding the beat of a world music, of a multicultural and multidimensional rainbow of shared awakening. A festival is at hand. It involves the freeing up what had become too dense, so concrete it really couldn't go on. The Sun is the one we can heed inside and outside; the Sun reveals what we have been missing and needing.

On the micro-level of each one's soul striving, there are challenges and difficulties in the realm of the Sun. All of these come down to the same thing. The Sun will not let you be. It is an ardent partisan. Insistently at all levels the Sun selects out what will serve the common future and eliminates whatever stands in the way.

Yes, the Sun is too cocky, too bold, too convinced of itself. Yes, the Sun won't listen to the sober counsel of other more grounded planets. Yes, the Sun makes us do and become more than we are ready for at any given time. Yes, the Sun exposes too much darkness too relentlessly for our taste.

The Sun is really a regent or representative of both the Christ Presence and every Christ-like being and force we could ever come upon in any tradition. What these forces have in common is a heart's path of redeeming this world's pain by embracing this world's promise fully and selflessly.

We meet the spiritual aspect of the Sun, the inner Sun, wherever we strip away the thin layer of separative pretense, and penetrate through to the blazing presence behind our hearts, the liberator and pure advocate of our complete awakening within this creation's boundless horizon. We embrace the Sun the most deeply and profoundly when we stand selfless to ourselves and meet our own brightness. This quality is there in everybody, to be fostered and not held off in any elite context whatsoever.

Our own little micro-Sun, our birth solar spark, starts out in life by being more of a hovering guest, a presence just out of reach. To incarnate the Sun is a life-long intensive initiation. All that brightness needs clarity of intention to make it viable in the thick of everything we meet and must work to transform. Clarity of intention becomes the foremost sign of a true solar initiation at work.

The only genuine concern we should have in relation to our solar spark is that it must come into substantive presence according to rightful timing. Each one of us has a built-in barometer that monitors this timing. This barometer must be respected, not overridden by exogenous factors. If we bring the Sun on too fast, it can burn out. If we bring it on too slow, we will not express our full potential in this lifetime. When the Sun comes on in Heaven's timing, it is an unmitigated blessing, an honor to behold and partake in.

The Sun bears a wisdom that is future generative. It knows effortlessly how to move through and beyond every contemporary trap. This transmission activates in our bodies and in our awareness. What it always says is: to walk onward, to sense those of spirit who accompany us, and to follow the deep heart track which wings us homeward.

Alpha Omega

In 1977, outer science recognized a new planetary body, or asteroid, or who-knows-what, which became known outwardly as Chiron. This name was taken to signify a wounded healer. Soon a narrow and tight interpretation was put on the workings of this new planet.

Many years later, outer science recognized that "Chiron" was part of a whole new system of planetary bodies. This served to make our focus on the new planet even more tentative and diffuse.

Let us now throw off these late twentieth-century blinders. The new planet or asteroid or new kind of planetary body can be called by its cosmic name, Alpha Omega. The title shows us where to look to expand our feeling for what this revitalized domain reveals in us.

The pulse of Alpha Omega is to tap two points in a field, to set up a resonating vibration between them, and to begin to introduce the full power of the counter pole into the most central workings of any given aspect of existence. We tap origin and destination, move between past and future as our primary polarity-weaver. From there it is open season on all the ways in which one side meets another side and polarization yields to reconciling and unifying action.

We begin to get an energetic feeling for our opposite gender according to its own way of being, not compared, not evaluated, not judged, not reacted to, just met freely and openly, inquisitively, with a need to know what is there. We go through a similar process with each facet of existence that previously felt as though it was foreign.

In the quintessential expression of Alpha Omega, we take this process one step further. As we grow accustomed to a shared world, a multiple existence, as we gain tolerance of chaos and more and more responsiveness to a chance in the midst of madness, a different kind of awareness reveals itself. At first, this new way of experiencing life seems to be almost too ideal, too optimal, too sanguine in its vision.

Then it happens. We suddenly get it on all levels at once that we are entering a different time zone, a very divergent sense of time altogether. There is space and breath within time. There is ample room within time for any and every development that needs to occur. Instead of time running out, Alpha Omega reveals a world where real time is ready to begin.

Previously, we assumed that the outer laws of science, based on surface observation techniques, were the holders, the carriers for collective reality. Under that regime we saw time mechanistically. Soon we even saw time as the most precious of commodities, running out fast. All this seemed commonsensical and realistic.

Through the cycles of Alpha Omega we gradually awake to a cosmic sense of time. Everything contains within it where it started and where it ends. These energy frequencies are active in the current field at any moment—so this moment becomes all of time held in a timeless poise. Every direction and world feeds into the moment. We then can unfold in freedom. There is no further reason to bind ourselves under fractional time contexts. We are able to claim this time as open. We don't have to rush. We can get there faster because "there" is "in," not ahead, beyond.

The first collective movement which bases itself upon an Alpha Omega sensibility is death and dying. Whether it is near-death experiences, the power of what happens as we lie dying, or our greater links with those who have died, the death-and-dying movement brings us into a light shining out of a dark tunnel, a heavy suffering, a long tragic and unredeemable domain. The new life of the newly dead, the greater link we can forge with them, and the remarkable way in which near-death experiences correlate with what is evolving upon the threshold now for us all—these forces become signal flares for a future where we do not shadow even death itself, or the life we live in Earth, or any polarity along the life-death continuum.

What has been emerging through the death edge in the last twenty years of the twentieth century enters the twenty-first century spread out into myriad movements and streams. Each of these bases itself on discovering a greater spaciousness, a stretch where previously all sides seemed shut tight against each other. The polarities which have underwritten the strife of modern times become transmuted into the mutual discoverers of how much we need one another (dead or alive, dead and alive) to have a complete readiness for what unfolds next.

In each one's personal chart, Alpha Omega points closely to the one spot where we can crack through our limited concepts and notions and come to a place of freely making room for what we previously scorned or despaired of.

Alpha Omega is our cosmic pulse of dispassionately witnessing how our lives look from the whole field at once. This new planet guides us to turn ourselves upside-down and inside-out. The one thing we can count on with Alpha Omega is that we will become more interesting to ourselves as we allow far more of life and death to be real and alive and part of our daily experience of this cosmos we have been born to witness. Then the habitation of the whole cosmos—at all levels, not just so-called I-am-alive ones—will become real in the way it already always is.

The Twelfth Life Stream

The Twelfth House

We live in darkness inside the Twelfth House. If we can honor what the darkness reveals, our existence is blessed by the fertilities of the dark. If we fear and shun darkness, it has a way of twisting and turning inside of us and making us susceptible to compulsive extremes and old stuck places interminably.

The course in darkness, the learning, the practice is always there when we walk through the Twelfth House. We may suppress it, but it accompanies us. What it most asks is that we breathe through every cell and sensation of ourselves, and that we keep allowing the multiplicities of existence to surge through us and not be blocked by any surface preoccupation.

The darkness initiates the one who can be in touch and in tune with a much deeper field of experience, pulling us beyond what we think about and see in front of us.

This deepening of capacity arises first as a longing, a fervent desire, as though from long ago and far away. We can't shake it. We can't explain what it's really about. To track it at all asks us to suspend rational faculties and enter the darkness within. If we do so, we will lose ourselves many times over and, as this happens, we will be fertilized and restored by the cycle and depth of the passage. Soon we will be able to move through ourselves and not be so densely packed in our being-stuff.

Most of our experience inside the Twelfth House will be subtle, strange, fascinating, compelling, and beyond the grasp of outward measure. Let us then submerge ourselves in the frequencies of the

Twelfth House rather than trying to fit them within any maps or concepts. Let us allow the Twelfth House itself to speak and to reveal its mysteries directly.

I am a trance. I hold the between spaces. I am responsible for keeping the record. My voice is a quiet one, but it runs deep. You can come into a few layers of me now. I will guide you through the maze.

What you meet first in me is an enigma, a riddle. You know that I hold menacing things, yet you can also sense that I offer immense treasures. You can come into these treasures if you can pass through your subjective hell—yes, that place where all those menacing things will be reflected. Would you like to try to go further?

As you enter upon me more truly, you can begin to sense all around you that whatever you have previously created is here as a possible world for you to be. If you died in ways that weren't complete and whole for you in another life, your initial feeling (as you go into these places) will be dread and horror, for we are bringing you back to where you got lost. If you died with an open heart and a ready will in another life, you will enter here feeling that there is great light in the darkness, and that what you come upon is already a part of you, just waiting to be claimed. After all, here you are; you got through, again.

What I can promise is that as you spiral in upon the inward circles of your being, drawing closer to the source, you will be able to recognize and unite with everything in you that you had forgotten and missed. I will be forthright with you right away: There will be a great cost involved. A great, great cost.

I am asking and demanding something of you in return. It is my right to do so. I will extract from you every ounce of self-importance. I will strip you bare of every self you thought you were. I will take away from you whatever you lean on as crutches and hiding places. I will not listen to reason.

My claim in here is that you have wandered so far out onto the shiny surface of the world that you have lost your bearings. I am charged with the task of bringing you back to your inner senses. And I know how to get you there.

What I do best is dramatize very convincingly all the most naggingly lost and stuck patterns you have ever identified yourself within. I make these feel inevitable, inescapable, as though they have always been there and there has never been a way out of them. This is intended to draw you into a deeper trance. Only from that place can I bring you a saving grace. Only then, when you are at last centered within an experience of something real and unbudgeable, can your real life begin.

Once you have taken on your share of the dark legacy, once you have swum awhile in the waters of Nepenthe, your lost self, your wandering soul will begin to come to you and ask for retrieval, plead for a new world to be in. Then your greatest tests will arise. Can you give to the lost inner ones a sanctuary, a place to grow and to thrive? Or will you deny their cry and their call?

I am the mistress of illusions. I am the bearer of mixed treasures. I take you where you would not go. I have an integrity and a conviction in all that I do. If you knew how long I've been here, how ancient I am, you would not be able to look away from me. I always let people off light. They only need to take up a layer or two of me at a time—that's my familiar pace.

If you should be a rare one who is stripped bare of self, I offer you free passage into the deepest conceivable journey in the world. There you can help and even save those lost in these waters.

Scorpio

When Scorpio is in active mode, all things change. A deeper core energy infiltrates—a subtler feeling tone. A dark and, in many ways, alien energy and awareness begins to suggest and imply that there is something more happening here. Scorpio intends to bring into the immediate situation all the undertones and overtones which we have skillfully filtered out in modern times. It is the nature of Scorpio to defy and stand against all surface human tendencies to outlaw and marginalize and scapegoat the hidden dark places. In Scorpio what others attend to is a given, and what others seek to get rid of is where the treasures and powers, the memories and breakthroughs lie.

The track which Scorpio navigates is forbidding to those who have forgotten what it means. There is a law, a pattern, a design which people associate with the Goddess and with the Earth as a living being; some correlate this with the Divine Mother energy or with an ancient future feminine power known as Sophia. That pattern inscribes (between the spaces where mind dwells) a web, a weaving, an intricate latticework of all living beings connecting at a deep-core hidden level. Scorpio is tracking that wilderness and is guardian to it, fierce maintainer of its ways.

The most awesome responsibility goes with this path, for Scorpio must shape-change into several different entities, become many worlds, often not overtly aware of one another. A great eagle-form roams the ethers and seeks the highest, clearest path forward, often with scant regard for the difficulties in getting there.

A dark scorpion energy slithers in the deep tenebrous spaces and destroys what is no longer holding up, making way for the shape behind a distant gleam. A lizard wanders through ordinary affairs, generating chaos and confusion, stirring things up while letting deeper layers through. A dove of spirit presides over all and makes sure we are serving the Great Mother's powers. A crone of the human kind sits in the cave and stirs her cauldron, chanting for there to be a return to heart essence in the land.

None of these shape-changing realms can be reduced to more typical ways of outer seeing. These are not psychological complexes. They are tied in with past lifetimes, past deathtimes, and the haunting places from which we all flee and within which we are fascinated. Far more, Scorpio involves a mutation toward the future. She is responsible for sustaining a shimmer on an alternative frequency, moving through what the surface civilization has destroyed. She tends that life flame as her fervent magisterial charge.

If we picture magic, shamanism, and the hidden worlds as Medieval, devilish, as delving in places we are all best off sealing over, the inherent strangeness of Scorpio becomes impenetrable. Why would anybody be that passionately intense about layers of existence so buried they are almost not here. Is Scorpio as perverse and wrong-headed as so many see her?

Only if science is perfectly correct and if the fundamentalist religions have their facts right…Only if the standard institutions of the twentieth century are really for the good, enlightened and clean….Only if the mainstream version of how it all is turns out to be accurate, true, and comprehensive….

If there is something dead wrong with the entire modern worldview and if the irrational harbors everything we have lost touch with, then Scorpio is onto something big. The Earth will awaken and soul will return.

The dreadful, bizarre, truly shadowy facet of all this is that we have gone as far as could be gone in the direction of excarnation from our Earth roots. Modern civilization pushes its shadow projection onto the Scorpio level. The mask is so thick, so heavy, so immobilizing that everything we fear and accuse comes into being. We call up from Scorpio a drastic rebellion, a destructive vibration. Scorpio proves that she is more intelligent than we would ever assume.

The ultimate victory of Scorpio is to bring the forbidden places into currency along a path that eclipses rage in fires of love. All those factions and long-built-up feuds dissolve into dust. An evolutionary wave hits Scorpio broadside. She comes to sense at the deepest levels that her being is only love and that everything she had shunned and known on her fabulous false tangents are integral parts of what she is called to love.

The Scorpio journey digs so deep into the soul that it can never stop at some position, some role, some way of feeling and perceiving that is inherited from the ancients. She is called to metamorphose, to transmute each and every ancient enmity into groundworks for regeneration into a new world. She is just beginning to ride the wave of what this might mean.

The extraordinary truth is that Scorpio ends up swallowing every history, myth, and soulscape. She has an ultimate bottomless appetite. What she craves is something new and different, something emergent and alive.

She may prevent her own liberation out of sheer orneriness. She may block others from a similar stance. On the other hand, she might just as well be the one to open the way to all. That is her sacred charge and the only thing that can gather all her resources together to do something worth dying for.

Pallas

We have tracked Vesta and Juno and Ceres through the asteroid belt previously. Now it is time to dive into Pallas. She holds the hidden keys to the whole subplanetary belt.

We shall first consider the nineteenth- and twentieth-century mass-manipulation version. Then we will allow the full dimension of twenty-first-century asteroid turnaround to take us on a different journey.

We have used Pallas so far to achieve a split between outer surfaces and inner depths. She has seized the territory of the other three asteroids as an outer sanctuary from the rumblings of the primordial depths. Pallas has pulled us hard toward the make-believe world, giving us a gut instinct for how to hang out in the official version and to keep all underworlds at bay.

From there the way of it gets pretty thick and gnarly. Pallas has warded off collectively all signs and evidence of hidden worlds resurgent. It has been the vintage anti-feminine asteroid, the betrayer of her sisters. What she seeks is a world free of her depth fears. She keeps pushing every terror and anxiety, dread and bleak memory onto the world around her and insisting that she be protected and preserved from the enactment of her own secret depths.

Pallas has made it very hard for any of us to move with our insides in confidence, trust, and faith. Having walled off the soul realms, she tries to generate an outer landscape that is intended to make all subtle dimensions obsolete. Her naiveté knows no bounds. She has actually come to believe that laws and taboos, subtle restrictions and considerations, can keep the dark away. At her most extreme of late, Pallas has entertained the omnipotent fantasy that each and all of us can be permanently in the free and clear and open, no hidden meanings needed here.

In our individual charts, Pallas has mostly served as veto power, the vote against living from within. She has been the enforcer of the social code at all levels, having exiled, scapegoated, marginalized, and subjected to extreme derision everybody in us who is outside the official program and likely to cause a ruckus. Our conditioning agent supreme, escapist Pallas gets in there when we are around eight to twelve years old and convinces us that we are entering upon a world where it will not be safe to bring with us anything that is charged, powerful, different, strange, or too much.

Pallas has been eroding us at very deep levels. She has gotten inside our psyche and insinuated the paranoid idea that all the places we have ever hung out on the inside are the problem and that worldly status is what we need and crave and must have. In her ravings, Pallas has been so collectively plugged in that we get jolts of her programming to keep us in line. Her maxim is: not entertaining outrageous notions which only get people in trouble.

Pallas' reign is at an end; she will lead the turnaround in the twenty-first Century from our modern witch hunts (in truth, the worst ever) to an all-embracing willingness to make room for whatever needs to unfold here. This will be Pallas' awakening, first individually and then collectively, to the simple reality that we *do* create from within our own personal souls all the heavens and hells we are living and that we can do the best job of ending our modern miseries by opening the doors and admitting these heavens and hells to play themselves. At this point Pallas' version need no longer be kept as volatile chaotic undertones, overtones, and reminders that there is *so much more to us* than we know. When we acknowledge it as it is, the danger inside us will release its constant outside threat and we will be in a safe universe—not a universe without danger but a universe whose dangers are not themselves maleficent.

Each of us have had a Shadow Essence which gave us every chance to lose ourselves, to enter the void, to be stripped of pretense and allowed to drift and dream and forget. Pallas had convinced herself throughout the nineteenth and twentieth centuries that this Shadow is the root of all evil and must be gotten rid of. Any Shadow Essence gets engorged when it is pushed under too far for too long. We became possessed by it, trying to eliminate its power while we were catalyzing and activating it unconsciously.

Twenty-first-century Pallas will be re-introduced to all the forbidden places. Yet they won't turn out to be ghoulish and scary. They will be the places we need to let go in order to return renewed. Pallas will mark the exploration, the discovery journey that lets us integrate what we have previously banished, what has previously dogged us with phobias and obsessions.

The asteroid belt is about to be sprung by galactic forces from the alien-abduction level of negative E.T.s into a spark for reweaving our part of this Living Earth. We will cease to feel a deep-down-under pressure to get out of this planet and to get rid of ourselves. As we are blessed with a cosmic renewing stream, each of our asteroids will begin to re-polarize itself from being dead set against us as living beings to offering us a path to walk that draws us right into our real connection with the Earth.

In sum, each asteroid really has been a plague, a pestilence, an abomination. Very few of us could overthrow their individual and collective tyranny. Yet the biggest shift in the New Millenium is that the extermination will be called off, the death dogs will be vanquished. We will have another chance, a deeper breath. For we have not been as far off course as we were led to believe. The notion of us as a failed species is yet another paranoid technocratic mirage, designed to lure us out of our depths, designed to get us to concede to surfaces. But a dose of deep reality will restore us to ourselves and reveal that we are (and always have been) spirit essence, deeply inwardly bright.

Biographical Embodiment
— through the example of —
Sara Lonsdale, Theanna Vivyen

CHAPTER 1

The Twelve Life Streams

— Sara Natal Chart —

The First Life Stream

Whether we view Sara through the lens of her Venus at birth in the end of the Twelfth House conjunct Pluto, or through the portal of her Mercury on the rise in the First House, with Sun and Juno at the end of the house, or we look toward the Taurean Heavenly Crown Signature, we will be seeing Sara clearly and resonantly in three synchronized ways through these diverse portals. If we now choose her Venus directly, it is in order to plunge in deep right away and let her destiny speak for itself in the language of the Twelve Life Streams.

Sara's Venus is in 12° Leo. The Chandra symbol is "The Mouth of the Amazon River." Sara traces her life's story back to its source. She balks heavily for a long time against the concept of past lives—for she is afraid that if she lets herself go back there, she'll get caught in an old place that her Pluto is constantly sourcing for her—and then indeed it does happen. What she feared comes true. The floodgates open to past life after past life. Each and every one of these contains dilemmas, issues that are still burning. A Venus at the end of the Twelfth House conjunct Pluto is all about feeling what you don't want to feel, experiencing what is too deep and strange to fit with who you were trying to be for others. The Leo In-Breath feels there's not enough clear space around here; everything is impinging.

Yet in truth, Sara's life begins when she starts to face her karmic legacy. She is not about happiness and all the easy things; she is desperate to retrace her steps and find who she really is after all. She knows quite consciously that she bears great mysteries inside of her and treasures she doesn't know how to tap. As she begins to remember and to realize and to fulfill that heart space, an inner resonance, a whole different quality of being shines through her outward form.

Sara unfolds a substantive depth of embodied will. In stark contrast to all previous attitudes and stances toward herself, this overflows into a brash confidence. Toward the end of her individual lifetime in the Earth, there emerges through Sara a quality, given her broodings and handicaps, wildly unlikely, as we shall see.

The Sara of late 1993, dying of cancer, reborning into the living spirit just as fast, is one who beams into each and every soul permission, encouragement, a breath of life. Her own message and way of bringing it across takes on archetypal resonance. People are drawn to her as never before. What they see and find is their own sharpest stirrings in a form they cannot resist.

At the peak of her powers at the end of her life, Sara commands close attention. What do we see if we move all the way inside the Sara who dies? We meet a fiery presence of one who has claimed a forgotten heritage of ancient wisdom and a life-force embodiment of that wisdom that all of us around her, are healed by and imprinted with permanently.

But for herself at the end, there is this flooding, this rapturous tumult. All destiny's futures are rushing into the now. All of who she will ever be again in any world is manifest—a voice, a fragment, an intonation. Yes, Sara is surrounded by spirits—and many of them are herself from future worlds greeting her, saying, "You have done it sister; you have come through!"

Sara smiles at the end just as she cried so at the beginning. She is ready at death for something more. Her Venus has shown her that she is a source presence, that she cannot be destroyed, and that everything in her is truly sacred. She is ready and she is willing. As we view the other streams, let us remember how it turns out.

The Second Life Stream

Sara is Virgoan. Her Second House Cusp is Virgo. Her Sun and Juno in Virgo reside at the end of the First House. Although she has Jupiter and Neptune and Alpha Omega all together in Libra in the Second House and her Vesta in Scorpio late in the Third House, it is indeed Virgo who wants to be seen now in all its rich complexity and inherent contradiction.

For Sara, to be Virgo in 17°— "An old bald woman talking to her dog"—is to be concentrated intensively upon the issue of individual integrity. She is her own watchdog, looking out for the best interests of the soul inside her. She wants to make sure, down to the finest detail, that she is establishing congruence between her inner soul and her outer expression. Though she knows this is an obsessive perfectionism, it matters tremendously to her. Nobody else has to live her life as she does. Nobody quite realizes the pains she must go to just to be here. Sara's nature at core is to overcome, to move through, is not to dawdle in any stases and norms. She forces herself, relentlessly in fact, to be good—and she is not good. She is every which way, as all souls are.

It gets very tangled up in here. Sara is able to take the Virgo path where it wants to go. This means that she will come to herself in the process of being a beacon to others—a best friend, a support system, a sounding board. But to come to herself will go against the grain of being a mother, a wife, a community member—tough choices. Inside her solitude, Sara will actually be seeking to draw upon its treasures. Her quest will center around excavating a lost self within a world that has no place for lost-self ventures. This tale is common, ordinary. Virgo is nothing special, nobody different. She just has to get it right somehow.

For herself, Sara experiences the Virgo twists and turns as home territory. Unlike most, she does not curse the Virgoan task and predilections. She needed this sign to come through with. It gives her so many virtues. Sara has the ability to do what she says she's going to do. She has a rare kind of companionable nature. She's a lot further in here than those around her ever are. Yet there is that Virgo problem.

Sara has to learn how to let go. For a very long time, this stops her cold. She hangs in there tightly—nobody must think badly of her. After being the ugly one left out, she becomes a cheerleader in high school. She learns to excel in everything she does. She is caught in one role, one self, one face.

Virgo gets identified within a fragment of itself and just stays that way for fear of the consequences involved in claiming a varied and unpredictable nature. Even for Sara, with all her courage and vision, the Virgoan trap is set. After giving so much away to those who want and need her to be their mainstay, she struggles mightily to make herself her own.

When a Virgo does let go, and learn to let go ever more deeply and finely as Sara certainly does, this becomes the very center of her life. She becomes one of those shape-changing beings who can become so many different ways and still be themselves. This is quite a stretch for Virgo. Sara learns to live on her edge. She thrives this way.

Eventually, the Virgoan struggle relents a bit. Humor holds sway. Detachment bears a certain weight of authority and conviction. Virgo has battled the mind down to the tiniest detail—and she comes away with the feeling that it really was all worth it—because her mind is her own at death. The life path was to become truly her own being on all levels. Sara does fulfill Virgo, its fiber of integrity.

The Third Life Stream

With the Moon and three asteroids in the Third House, this Stream gives Sara one big set of headaches. Forget Neptune and Sagittarius; they are not major factors. Let us merge into Sara's deepest dilemmas and see if we can empathize with what a Twentieth Century woman had to go through in order to be in tune with the many voices clamoring for her attention.

Subjectively, hyper-personally, the Sara Moon in 21° Libra—"A magician wearing a live snake for a belt"—experiences each and every day with strong emotional energy around it, charges of all the most troublesome kinds, alerting her that she is not doing what she is here to do, she is not being the one she is here to be. Apparently every outer factor in her immediate world is gathered into a conspiracy to make sure that Sara will not break through. Her feeling of engulfment by external social forces is so drastic that she usually believes that there is something mentally wrong with her. She just cannot be at peace with the one in her who shows up everyday—the one who is captured by external magic, is cut off from the only magic that is real.

All three asteroids seem to chime in: It is like this for everybody. It is best to resign yourself to whatever you are up against. This world is not ever going to change, not really. For Sara, these voices are compelling, distinct, pervasive. They compromise her ability to feel connectedness to anything vital. While tending to become mechanical, formal, rigid in outer duties, she feels when she gets up every morning that she faces insurmountable obstacles that day. Her body is hurting. She is tired and drained. And so it goes, day after day.

Is there any place that Sara can turn in the midst of this kind of syndrome? Well, it takes an extreme crisis, a life-or-death situation to bring relief here. The coping behaviors, the going along with conditioning is pretty dense and habitual. Yet cancer tumors have a way of getting your attention and holding it there.

The collective quickening to a future pulse that is now arising in the Third House comes through to Sara right away when she starts to empower herself to tackle her own cancer by inward means. A great wave of real magic enters her life. And this holds sway throughout her battle with cancer.

Sara is suddenly off the hook with others and herself, at least in terms of making a living, shrugging off her illnesses and injuries, and showing up as an easy person to be around. For Sara, this shift is decisive. Everything else is very secondary. She needs to feel justified, freed up, given the chance to claim her own soul's longing and agonies.

Throughout the cancer battle Sara mostly inhabits a shadow realm. She is learning to go deep, to stay with her pain, her emotions, her personal experiences. But even more sharply she is discovering how to honor her own subjective mind and emotions, how to be a deep inner witness to her process, one who doesn't fly above, but instead lands again and again far below.

In the thicket of that cancer battle, the Third House takes an even more radical turn. Sara has been one of those who feels habitually very guilty, very ashamed. She assumed it was because she was cheerful when others were in heavy states and she assumed she must be superficial. Now this grip is relinquished. Sara discovers that she is naturally resilient, buoyant, endlessly resourceful. With the stigma removed, she can be a bright spirit in the depths and never apologize again. For Sara sees through things into the other side, and her vibrancy pulls her right through—even in death struggle.

The Fourth Life Stream

Scorpio at the Earth Root. Moon and Pluto already explored. The Earth under Pisces. Let us dive inside the Earth under Pisces at the end of the Seventh House and tap the portal of Pisces to reveal the most ultimate, essential things about Sara.

The Earth under Pisces degree is 17° —"A baby kangaroo in its mother's pouch." Down under there, Sara is dreaming—she is in the kangaroo dreaming. An aboriginal Australian lifetime comes up here. She was tracking the deep-water dreaming with others in her tribe. Then she lost the link with the her clanmates and drowned. Suddenly she found herself in another existence altogether. Beings of a greater consciousness and stature were communing with her and preparing her for a colossal task to come. This time away was the most cosmically charged experience Sara had ever taken up.

The Earth under Pisces remembers the drowning at a deep cellular level. There was another drowning—voluntary—in ancient Hawaii, the lover lost, the world no longer worth staying in. An Oahu beach—just going out and out forever. Many drownings in many lives of different kinds. This Earth-under carries the deep hidden message that each human connection will end with a sense of loss and severance that can never be healed.

This Earth-under soul mood runs deep, runs far. It generates a soul melancholy of a sort that is rarely indulged by Sara. She stays choleric to herself, seeking mastery always. But her wounded-child, her traumatized ancient, timeless soul is lost out there somewhere and doesn't know what happens next. A certain fatalistic, stark resignation jells protectively. The psychic faculty, the multi-sensory attunement of Pisces becomes pivotal in Sara's life.

Her subtle feelers reach in to each other soul she encounters. She needs to know them, to sense their ache, their longing, their desperation, their hidden quest. She feels so deeply drawn to the lost soul in each and every one—and she also feels (with the other fish) so sharply pulled away, entirely resistant to and reactionary against people's weaknesses and susceptibilities.

It is this psychic tug of war between the most profound empathy and the most wrathful judgment that becomes her soul drama—the negative against her positive—between Sara and each one she loves. Playing into what is expected, each other blocks her from her own soul depths. Many ways at different times, the arena of relationship is saturated with undertones of sympathy and antipathy, love and hatred, the most soul-stirring allegiance and fidelity versus a sense of abandonment and betrayal.

Sara is psychically charged within these depths. She is not shut off or tuned down. Quite the opposite! Her timeless experience is that she remains sensitized, acutely present to the karmas and their outworking. The baby kangaroo must stay at attention and feel it all and know that what arises is coming to something not yet conceivable, pulling at both partners with an insistent, creaturely tug, as if the whole world depended on it.

The one experience of Sara's Earth-under Pisces is being pulled toward a future death that puts all the past deaths in an entirely different perspective. She must swim toward a free death and clear out the sludge of all those drownings and submergences. This is an impossible task, yet it is the only one left for her to take up.

For all those Piscean infinity fears and corrosive doubts, the Earth-under Pisces for Sara is a vital link. It brings her back to where she must go if she wants to be free. Though Pisces is exquisitely painful at this level, inside the agony somebody who is brand new is borning.

The Fifth Life Stream

We will catch up to Saturn when we get to the Twelfth Life Stream. Sara's Earth under we have just fathomed. She has Dragon's Tail in Capricorn in the Fifth House—but it is Leo that now calls to us to be viewed as a whole. The In Breath Signature or Rising Sign is Leo, with Venus and Pluto and Mercury all there as well. What is Leo truly for Sara?

Sara is rabidly intent upon optimizing the gifts of the sign of Leo for herself. She fully emerges into these capacities later in life. But Leo is with her from the beginning—this drive, this purposive gleam of resolve to pull herself together and to become her truly best self in this lifetime.

Leo can be the most rigorous of signs. For Sara, it definitely forges her. Her In Breath Signature is 18° Leo—"A rose bush. Many buds, but no flowers." She lives with a promise, an aspiration, a vapor. Whatever she must do to get through she will bear with all of her being. What acutely does she seek to become?

She has no clear idea. The ideal image eludes her altogether. There is no definite goal. Instead, there is a powerful process unending. Leo has such radically deep issues around self-validation. How can Leo at this kind of juncture, where nothing is ever known out ahead, be able to believe in herself and not only stay with herself but abide with conviction and gladness?

Sara's personal shadow is that she cannot do it. She has been through too much karmically to be naïve to her own shortcomings. In fact, she berates herself constantly for being such a coward.

Leo often sidles up against an unbearable conflict between backing her inner self forcefully and steadily and being in friendly, open, generous connections with others. For Sara, this conflict is back-breaking. She can never resolve it. Her heart is too vast. Yet her intent to be true to her purpose and task is also fierce.

The only option open to Sara is to live authentically with her foundational ambivalence. She must go against herself and then come back to that same self a thousand times. But primarily she must hold open a space, at first one that is very small. In this self-beholding place, she is meant to witness the claims of the world upon her in their legitimacy—and then she must also bear witness to the equally strong and legitimate claims of her own deep inward soul upon the path of evolvement. She must inch toward herself, while keeping a broader avenue open and free to the world of others.

Sara will not accept anything less than this from herself. And, as we'll explore in the Seventh Life Stream, her Mercury in 30° Leo does get her where she needs to go. Along the way, one special agony haunts Sara and never lifts.

It is her innermost will to give of herself creatively in a major life work. She is an artist—a healer. Though she puts in much substantive work toward every phase of this aspect of her life's expression, she cannot be the one she sees inside—this never quite comes true.

For Sara, the sacred arises when she is empty and almost bereft. She is seeking no less than Christ and she will not find Him through any wondrous self-fullness. When she tries on (for size) New Age teachings, she flatters herself a while (as many do) that she can have it all. But her deep soul doesn't identify with the fulfillment of any separative way of being. It is ultimately true that for Sara, Leo is a testing sign, leading to her true selfless nature, and giving very little reward along the way for being a shining light. This humbles her, keeping her in good shape for her spiritual journey still to be described. Sara burns through herself to her own satisfaction.

The Sixth Life Stream

With a Juno less than prominent, an Aquarian Out Breath Signature, and a Capricorn Sixth House cusp with no planets in the Sixth House, this Life Stream is not a pivotal influence for Sara. Yet we will take up the Capricorn Sixth House cusp from a whole different level. Time to dive into karmic starwork.

The Sara Capricorn cusp is 20°—"Many different perfumes carried by a breeze." Guidance showed Sara (repeatedly throughout the 1990s) a key past lifetime as a classical Mayan in the highlands of her people at a time when they were in the peak of their glory. Sara was shown that this lifetime was held within the Sixth House as something to be worked out intensively again if there was to be a catching up with self and moving forward.

On the outside, Sara's Capricorn cusp functioned as a dutiful and stern participant in immediate tasks and objectives. However, the subconscious mind that runs so rampant in the Sixth House became a seedbed of infinitely suggestive currents, vibrating, scything through and leaving their mark. Sara's subtle mind was replaying odors, visions, tangible events that happened so long ago. This layer was stopping her cold in her tracks.

Retracing the lost pathway, Sara became aware that once upon a time she was at the center of an advanced group of souls who were guided to unite themselves with the gods and goddesses in order to seed a greater stage of human evolution. There were austerities, initiations, ordeals. Few ascended to the peaks at the end. One of these few was carrying an internal twist, deeply hidden, that would undermine what was intended to arise between humanity and the gods. At the crucial moment, Sara misjudged her own capacities. The chance slipped from her grasp, back into the void. When petitioners returned empty-handed from their many years of most arduous efforts, everybody knew that the Mayans would be strewn to the winds, that the greatest destiny of these people would not be fulfilled.

Sara had taken this defeat upon herself utterly. It was a burden she could not lightly release. During the first year after she was shown this scenario directly, she developed cancerous tumors and became subject to her body's excarnational forces. No matter how hard she tried to come to grips with Mayan karmas, they were just too big for her—until a massive event shifted the balance.

In September and October 1992, Sara walked into Haleakala Crater in her homeland of Hawaii. Her Sixth-House body was not up to the task. Almost there, her Capricorn knees gave out completely. She had to be supported the rest of the way. She could not walk out again. In a series of miraculous events she was brought out of there on a donkey.

On this return trek a switchback area marks where the mountains become formidable, the weather most often stormy, and donkeys long to go off the trail, even if it kills both the animal and the rider. Sara found herself almost killed at just about every turn of the road. It was there she finally confronted the one in her who balked at everything, who defied authority, who respected nobody—the place where she was crimped. She knew that to get out of there alive, she had to be that donkey and blend with why it refused to stay on the path.

After that pilgrimage, Sara was willing to admit how wrong she had been, yet how right she was. She was wrong to go against the sacred in self out of sheer orneriness. She was wrong to defy the world's sacredness from her own immobile will. She was right to bring herself through this and embrace everybody's experience along these lines. Beyond right and wrong, Sara could be with herself upon her journey and know the rightfulness, beyond doubt's shadows.

The Seventh Life Stream

Mercury will show us who Sara is as a social being. Aries is not a strong sign in her. Having explored Earth under the Seventh House, let us inquire into her Mercury as pivotal life signature.

Mercury is on the rise in 30° Leo—"A woman sprinkling rose water in the four corners of a room." The fixed star Regulus locates right here. This is where the lessons of Leo are reaped. But what is this Mercury able to show us, beyond the usual astrological levels?

Sara is curious, inquisitive, is in each and every situation wondering who she is, who this other one is before her, and what their connection might really be. Contrary to the clichés, she really, truly wants to know, needs to know. Sara's existence depends upon being oriented in relation to others in all dimensions.

Above, in the spirit light, she must sense her way into why we meet, what is our karma, our shared destiny, where can we go with this encounter? Below, in depths of subtle consciousness and abyssal feeling, she tunes into the subcurrents and steers clear of false entanglement at every turn. On the In Breath, she seeks, especially wakefully, to stay with herself in the full spectrum of who she can be here and now. Then, on the Out Breath, she finds the precise place where we avoid each other, and where we come together despite ourselves.

Sara's self-appointed task is to tell the tale, to be the narrator, to witness and observe as though she had to stand in for the Divine Presence. Imbedded within this task is another. This hidden task dominates the recondite corners of Sara's awareness, corners which are attentive and vigilant. She must not only tell the tale correctly and in the largest context, she must also face what is holding things up here. She cannot turn away.

The latent task spins a much deeper, more ultimate tale. Sara is perpetually given the most convincing and persuasive pictures and demonstrations of where each one is stuck and also where each blocks the other. The most painful part is that she is implicated all the time—she is one of those who is caught and cannot connect as intended.

Yet Sara must continue unflinchingly just to see it as it is—a client, the one she loves, herself, a friend, a family member. What keeps people apart becomes the true study of her life. Accumulating evidence reveals that people now cannot and will not find each other. Gender and other polarity karmas turn them into categories for each other. The living being itself is unavailable, not intimately present; it has already gone somewhere else and cannot be hailed.

As with each and every other strange and impossible task Sara takes on, this one is seen through to a startling conclusion. Eventually, Sara discovers that if only she changes her stance, others actually, even unconsciously, will take the cue.

In her head, Sara had assumed, as so many do, that there was no living feedback loop, no psychic conversation, that she was on her own and unlikely to get much response, no matter what she did. Yet in the end she proved decisively to herself (and to spirits looking on) that her own creationary radiance, her life will had the current to change peoples' minds about what can move between beings. The leap she took was to give herself permission to make a fool of herself in every moment by stepping out of line and bringing a living impulse to dance, no matter how preposterous or unlikely, no matter what anyone thought.

The embodiment of this Mercurial resolve in the last weeks of Sara's life was complete. She opened lives everywhere she went. She even insisted on bringing worlds together that were, by seeming cosmic fiat, inalterably apart.

Sara had been desperately witnessing the worst news about people for a long time. Then she started telling the good news and (surprise) people listened. They just plain listened.

The Eighth Life Stream

The sign of Libra, with five planets in it at birth, wants to be unveiled now. Sara has no planets in the Eighth House, and we will meet with her Mars in the Eleventh Life Stream. So let us turn Libra inside out, to match Sara's life experience.

Libra moves between the poles of too much ego to meet what is really happening and too little real inner presence to give Libra a path through the metamorphoses that arise. For Sara, both these extremes become places she is called upon to awaken. Each turns out to be a dream, an absence, a trance.

The Libra with too sharp an egoistic quality of expression runs wild and free in Sara's world. Her Moon in Libra in the Third House pushes for getting away with outrageous impulses. Most of these are projected and played out by others. Sara provokes those most open to it to acting out her own errant impulses. Throughout her lifetime, this dynamic proves to be so strong that eventually its elusive way of sabotaging Sara becomes self-evident; she can no longer have fun at her own expense.

The Libran who recedes and dissolves and is never really there in what is unfolding on the outside turns out to be the fulcral key for Sara in her own self-scourings. She keeps tracing it back, coming up empty-handed. For months, Sara believes, in the midst of her cancer journey, that there really is nobody home, that her own personal soul is among the missing. *There is really nobody home.*

This very point represents falling for the seductive allure of the absent, weak Libra. And eventually, Sara starts to get it. She catches glimpses of the extent to which seeming to be gone has served her throughout this lifetime. What she was shrugging off was the heavy responsibility of Saturn square her Moon saying, "Hey, girl, when are you going to show up here?"

Finally catching up with the anonymous and helpless side of Libra that felt enmeshed unbearably, Sara brought the full power of her Jupiter/Neptune/Alpha Omega triad in Libra to the aid of a more latent quest. Sara had to get to the bottom of each and every syndrome she was confronted by, inside and out. But the hardest tracking came with the side of Libra that *could not be here at all.*

Sara's laser-sharp self-awareness, put to the ultimate test, came through brilliantly here. She simply discovered, for herself and all the other Libran recessives, that her heart was not in it because she felt rejected not just by parents and siblings, but by every living creature she ever met. And what was at the root of this heavy-duty, bone-weary belief?

Sara found that, under strain and pressure at a key juncture of her early life, she had rejected herself totally and blindly in a fury against herself. She hated that she was absorbed in a situation that was to her pathetic and useless and seemingly termless. When she went after herself big and hard and ruthless, she met reverberations of this same feeling tone in each and every other one, who would be bound, according to the self-rejecting instinct, to feel the same way about her.

What could Sara do once she found the cure of her life's worst syndrome? Nothing! This was one she had to accept and give over to the gods. The ability to care about her own lost child had atrophied and she was not about to pretend anything additional at this late date. Too long in a stupor, she was going to ride its wraith home.

Yet as soon as Sara placed upon the altar her feeling of not being able to get any further with her own personal soul wound, spirit forces acted with sweeping powers of intervention. Sara was shown on the inside that she had taken this pattern on for the sake of everybody and that she could let it go with equally gentle ease.

The Ninth Life Stream

Uranus is the strongest planet in Sara's natal chart, leading a pattern of five signs occupied, which we call the Trailblazer. Capricorn is minorly strong, and the Ninth House is very weak. But Uranus is endlessly worth awakening into in all its levels.

Sara's Uranus is 18° Gemini— "A book with blank pages." This degree of the Zodiac is a bottomlessly receding point, or a spiral rising to infinity. For Sara, it means that her whole soul stands before her as starkly as can be, yet she has no attitude or stance, nothing to say or do about it. Instead, she must become a pure witness in the most advanced sense. To do so requires her to rise level by level, self-schooling in a manner arduous and rewarding at every stage.

Sara keeps uncovering at each coil of the infinite spiral a greater spirit pressure, an accompanying breath. At first, she adopts this only within a religious context, later expanding it into esoteric understanding. As even this is far from sufficient, Sara quests onward.

In 1983, coming upon Kay Ortmans and her Wellsprings path, Sara learns that beings on the inside of life, called the dead by those who don't know them, are willing and able to give energy and awareness to those who connect with them through a lively material and bodily interchange. The mutual impregnation between spirit and world gets revived in Sara even from her ancient Maya downfall. She starts to trust the Living Spirit to be right there with her, vibrantly in tune with her destiny, showing what she needs to see.

In 1986, more directly receptive to spirit sources, Sara and her life-mate come into a resonance with guiding energies that are as sobering as they are renewing. The beings Sara contacts will not let her get away with any of her famous self-important notions.

It is these guiding beings who shine such a consistent, persistent light upon Sara's wakeful true being that her Uranus comes alive as never before and takes up a scepter of co-creation. This passage holds her aloft within it for the rest of her days.

Within this compass, Sara ultimately sees and knows herself as she truly is. This becomes her greatest shock. For seven years before epiphany, the spirit sources have been pouring into Sara a reflective awareness revealing her vital significance, juxtaposed to the perpetual reminders that she is as nothing. Just as the cancer tumors spread and the death energies were approaching more closely, Sara realized from within herself that everything she had been shown was correct in literally every detail. She then spent a month in existential shock. She recovered from the shock for another month. Then she came alive and was suddenly in the clear and true. There were no veils around her, no buffers left anywhere.

In those last weeks, Sara became a wayshower for the species—in her timing and after death. The single most unmistakable impression that beams through her Uranian sensibility is the fervent conviction—spoken, written, and shared with each and all from that moment forward—that life in this Earth is infinitely precious, that each one of us is true and beautiful beyond our ken, and that we have the chance in this phase of evolution to become every ounce of who we truly are, right here in this world. These are conditions perfect for awakening.

Sara goes out the top of her chart, out the Crown, as she dies. A great light being comes for her. She reaches to Him and they travel onward. One of those attending hears Sara say inside, "Do not fear for me—I know the way."

The Tenth Life Stream

The sign of Cancer is the very strongest influence of all in Sara's natal chart. We have already explored her Uranus late in the Tenth House. Her Ceres is a minor factor conjunct the Root. Let us take up the cosmic journey of the sign of Cancer in its most dramatic terms.

Sara is a soul covered over by outer form and possessed by an overwhelming impulse to throw off her disguise and be done with limitation. Her Mars, Dragon's Head, and Saturn in Cancer take on a thick layering of outer form limitation. Thus, Sara challenges herself to cut through a bombardment of roles, ancestral overlays, and rational mind concepts of what is rightful and what is truly necessary among outer reckoning.

Her progress through these multiple layers of programming is sluggish. To Sara's inner eye, it is so excruciatingly slow that it is barely movement at all. Is she getting anywhere? Why is it so hard to traverse beyond her own pervasive habit of becoming what everybody needs to see on the spot and then not knowing why she feels so terrible and out of touch?

Sara does have one thing in Cancer territory going for her, one thing rare and tremendously helpful. She can tap a lineage of her own prior lifetimes before she fell into the traps of the modern ego. Her Council of Elders is a complete circle of women and one man who have been through their own long ancient lives in this planet and have learned to stay with the process until it turns around just by sheer tenacious willingness to see life's lessons through.

Always the Council of Elders, working in a superconscious or overmind realm, have been revealing to Sara that she has it in her to outlast any and every syndrome, and that she will be given all the help she needs at critical points along the way. This sacred instruction informs Sara's life from the Crown above and grants her a certain timing grace of meeting each destiny challenge in rightful inner timing to take it up.

Because Sara is demonstrating in her whole life's path a quintessentially contemporary soul experience, she cannot lean back upon her Council of Elders and other spiritual helpers for some elitist special treatment. She must in her own personal soul renew the taproot, come to everything again from a place of immediate hunger and thirst. This is vital because Sara has agreed to confront her own most resistant layers as they unconsciously arise, penetrating through to wisdom only *after* exhausting the ignorance patterns she tries out endlessly.

Nonetheless, the Cancerian dispensation in Sara's greater destiny finds a way to crack open the densest shells and to emerge from these into a zone of authoritative presence. Sara forever seeks to serve, to teach, to help, to mediate the difficulties all around her. She comes to this point after being a Waldorf teacher, a mother and a homemaker. Her touch lights up; her healing powers manifest in her massage therapy. On several sessions she is allowed to transmit, when she is healthy enough, a stunningly regenerative force, shifting a number of human destinies.

At the end of her life, Sara is a master in the Cancerian realms. A Divine Mother, she has become capable of holding such a big space open that all of the collective swoops in as one organism. Quan Yin energetics are there, rippling through Sara's presence. They communicate to the world through Sara that all shall be held within the Mother's Embrace, that the world is safe, and that each one can trust absolutely in the Mercy of the Mother.

The Eleventh Life Stream

Sara has very strong Gemini in her, her Sun powerful in her chart. Alpha Omega in its conjunctions with Jupiter and Neptune is also ripping along. Yet it is the Eleventh House influence that we shall tap in order to explore Mars conjunct Dragon's Head in Cancer as the guiding star for her entire destiny.

The Sara Mars is quite a story in its own right. Its degree is 2°—"A bunch of iron keys." Sara indwells this realm purely. She holds within her own desire nature many keys to the future. These lead her forward, with the help of the Dragon's Head or Dragon's Breath. Sara becomes a visionary, one who sees beyond and knows how to get there. This is the place with which Sara wrestles so relentlessly. What is it she cannot quite claim or embody in her Mars genius?

Sara's Mars has no sympathies, no sentiment, not even a caring for who anybody is, where they are stuck, what they are dealing with. Her Mars feels with a rage only, a passion and abandon, that each and every one can and must overthrow their apparent constraints and become who they truly are, as ultimately intended. No matter what Jupiter square this and other reasonable influences might caution, the Sara Mars will not back down from the visionary stance that we *can* and *will* become all that we are, that what is in our way is trivial and absurd.

Why is Sara's Mars so adamant about this and what is it in her that stands back from this Mars in horror and cannot bear to live out its consequences? Mars in the Eleventh House grasps something others miss. It knows with unsympathetic glare that everybody around here needs to be pushed and pulled beyond their limits if anything's going to happen. However, such a Mars inevitably must first apply this lesson to the self. There it will confront a massive wall of resistance.

The personal soul says to such a Mars—"If you demand of me my utmost surrender, you will have to come in here after me. By the time I get through with you, you will have a feeling for what I go through and why I can't just drop it all when you come flying by." In Sara, this response and reaction feel unacceptable. She will not back down, yet she cannot inhabit her own Mars. She is caught between a fiercely firm vision and set of standards and a weakness comparable to any she meets in others.

The intimate politics of the twentieth century would dictate here that Sara back down from her wild-eyed insistencies and descend and join the rest of us in our common plight. Sara does not do this. Past lifetimes of conviction and a lineage in this lifetime of standing by high principles combine to hold her fast within her Mars position, unable to shift the balance. There is still one stop to take.

Sara discovers in her final death process that her cue to shoveling out the garbage faster than it comes in, to keep living through the cancer death as long as possible, is indeed to stand before herself with the most uncompromising inner gaze and insist that she not succumb to the extraordinary temptation to submit to the passivities of malignancy and death.

A moment toward the end illustrates this rightful defiance. She has put herself in the emergency room of the local hospital in order to get her bearings. They give her a much stronger drug than she is accustomed to. Twenty minutes after taking it, we imagine that the painkiller has got the better of her this time. Sensing that feeling, Sara shrugs off the drug as if it were nothing and becomes more lucid than ever. Her deep, dark eyes gaze at us with great amusement. She has again overthrown the limits. In her Mars, there is no need for any such excuse.

The Twelfth Life Stream

Scorpio is the Earth Root Signature for Sara. Pallas is conjunct her Moon in the Third House. The Twelfth House contains Saturn, Pluto, and Venus. We shall finish this natal chart exploration with her Twelfth House.

Here we must confront past lives and the realm of death itself. Each of these demands far more space than we can give it. A few words must suffice.

The key past lifetime for Sara, here as an overtone in the Twelfth House, is one in the Celtic Isles closely involved with Merlin and a circle that gathered around both him and her. The outstanding karma from that legendary lifetime involves a gut feeling, far deeper than we ever usually go in our self-process, that Sara cannot trust herself, dare not lean at all upon internal resources and the treasures she bears within her. Instead, the conviction is that urgent, critical matters, when they arise, must be in some form denied, avoided at any and all cost. Sound familiar? It must have resonated deeply with her soul.

Sara is adept, through her Saturn, in pushing out of her space all

138

crucial karmic matters. She turns these into a personal drama that she drains of its mythic significance. This strategy is intended to make her demands upon herself unable to stick. Sara gets so good at this that nobody and nothing can get at her at a deep effective level—all is deflected for later.

The working out of this syndrome is a key to Sara's miraculous turnaround. Stated with brutal frankness, Sara finds during her cancer battle that she has no further place to stand and that, when it comes right down to it, she is unwilling to protect herself. Instead of stonewalling further, she succumbs, entirely gives over, to her own and everybody else's surprise. Then she says: "I had to come out."

Dying proves to be the ultimate and essential journey in the Sara lifetime. She taps death's power to an extent and in a way we humans have forgotten how to enact—and actually haven't been in touch with for thousands of years. How did she do this?

The Sara Pluto in 11° Leo—"A boy removes a thorn from his foot" —centers her death journey at just about the deepest level there is. Uncovered are her own ancient Egyptian trainings in walking the edge between life and death, weaving these together in a combination different from any that have been since that time. The Plutonian key is to fuse with the death fires while retaining an indestructible core of presence that is *under,* rather than over, and therefore holds itself in there, even in the most extreme mortality throes.

In her dying process, Sara is consistently, eerily self-observant and self-mastering. She does this from a deep-earth quickening that only those who have partaken in alchemy and magic remember in their cells. Yet Sara insists at every juncture that what she is doing everybody can do. What does she mean by this really?

Death is the ultimate equalizer. Sara discovers only in dying that the pivotal quality seeing her through this, as incredible as it is, is not incredible at all; it is basic and universal and accessible. As long as she will not turn against herself, nothing anywhere can harm her. Even death has no fangs, no sting, if the one dying embraces within their death as the ultimate expression of who they are and affirms in the actual death process their ability to value themselves in the very moment they seem to be losing everything. Of course, once wide open, she can be nothing other than herself.

Sara finds dying and death to be her deepest friends, her companions. They guide her toward life. She dies willing to return in some miraculous new way. And because her desire is pure, her wish is granted, and her death becomes the starting point for another tale.

THEANNA VIVYEN
PRENATAL EPOCH
DECEMBER 5, 1944

CHAPTER 2

The Journey After Death into Rebirth Among the Living

— Theanna's Prenatal Epoch —

The Ninth House

Afterr Sara's death, her destiny metamorphosed into a direction unique and more cosmically whole than deaths have tended to be during this materialistic era. She died into the whole cosmos at once, and she asked that she be given an assignment right away, a task that could tap the power of her dying and death for everybody. What she asked was granted to her.

She was able then to return to dwell in part amongst the living. That part started out being small but would gradually grow through the soul bond with her mate, William. Two weeks after dying, Sara returned into the subtle body of William. The moment this happened, she became Theanna, who is willing to be as a god or goddess. He became Ellias, the light-bearer from the stars, piercing all other veils and disguises.

During Sara's earthly lifetime, before getting together with William, she had lived strictly by her birth chart. Then she had wrestled between the karmas given at birth and an entirely different entity, seeking to be born within and through her. For ten years, the old Sara could not give way; yet somebody in her, revealed by the Prenatal Epoch or Cosmic Conception chart, was seeking rebirth and struggling to emerge.

At the end of the Sara lifetime, the essence-being, the Theanna one, was already here amongst us, constantly consuming the last Sara karmas, yet palpably a whole different being. When Theanna emerged after death, her path with Ellias and into all of life could suddenly be tracked, in a highly discrete way, through the Prenatal Epoch chart.

Sara had died into the Crown, had gone out the top of her chart. Theanna now returned through the Crown and could thus travel backwards through the houses of the Prenatal Epoch. It was this journey we shall now track. We are concerned not so much with its revelations concerning life after death as with what occurs when a twice-born returns amongst us and gives of her essence in a concentrated dosage through others.

From December 1993 to June 1994, the Ninth House journey was fulfilled. The house cusp is 18° Aries—"A jellyfish." Theanna was bearing within her a vital current, but this had to be metabolized through the body of Ellias. For the first months he struggled to be present for such a potent transfusion. But his body was needing love and physical presence of the feminine to match frequencies with what was happening so beautifully on the inside.

During the early months of 1994, the friend who had united with Sara's death shifted into being Alita, an inwardly luminous essence, and she then closely accompanied Ellias in his efforts to bring Theanna all the way through into the Earth. Magic, alchemy began to unfold at a very deep level. We received Theanna to dwell amongst us and to bring her concentrated dosage of cosmic truth into our midst. The blazing, pioneering presence of Theanna was so strong and steady on that she brought awakening and renewal to all who could be with her. Her emanation spread through Alita. Ellias engaged in the pure witnessing of something wildly unlikely, yet absolutely real—more real than real.

The Eighth House

From June to December 1994, Theanna's miraculous penetration into life was consistently transformative. The cusp degree for this house is 18° Pisces—"White lilies blooming alone in the shade." This was happening of course on an interior level. Theanna came to us mostly within our own soul and body, although there were many external encounters with her as well. Much of the time she felt almost too close to be met. Theanna was starting to mold us to be very different kinds of creatures, encompassing much more of the future, much less of the past. As this process emerged, it rapidly became something we could not deny or relativize.

Alita started this initiation with lots of help from Theanna, Theanna as a whole different being. We learned with Alita that we could bring a healing impulse deep into the physical realm as needed. A very intimate miracle, it started a different momentum.

A comet was approaching Jupiter and about to hit that planet mid-July with a massive, detonative force. Despite official scientific denials, we knew this event was radically going to impact life in the Earth. We took our first major collective assignment at this time—for we had to be there together when the initial impact reached the Earth, and we needed to take it completely through us right away to help minimalize the damage factor in the planet. We collaborated with Deep Earth beings in order to fulfill what was intended. This was almost too strong a demonstration of our healing, transformative capability. Stunned by its simultaneous cataclysmic and epiphanic nature, afterwards we needed to integrate the experience for a while.

In the Fall of 1994, we travelled to Alaska together. An immensely pivotal previous lifetime for Theanna had unfolded there where she had been a native man in the days when the Inuits (or Eskimos) were at the height of their free culture. She had come to the Earth in the truest terms of incarnation there, in the pure ethers of the Northern realms.

During the Summer, friends closely linked with Theanna had gathered together and brought her into their midst by a special stone. She guided them into extraordinary group explorations through the unknown. We went to a singular spot in Alaska to complete the mission. The women had uncovered a local earthlock condition, a blockage of true spirit presence, apparently the effect of a darker influence at work.

When we arrived, our assignment together was to track down this detrimental influence to its strongest pulse, and there perform, instructed by Theanna, an unusual kind of exorcism. Her ritual embraced why the darker spirits had come and what their work there was; it released them from needing to carry it on any longer in that way.

During the Alaskan venture Ellias became attuned to a three-energy, a triad essence. Theanna was a shared living organism who wanted to guide Alita and him through. From that point forward we attempted to embody this bright intraterrestrial essence. Because we had received in Alaska an especially subtle transmission of Theanna, we were empowered to act. Major destiny challenges lay ahead.

The Eighth House journey shifted our focus completely from immersion in the heights to soul needs everywhere. We had to become attuned to the Earth's call.

The Seventh House

From December 1994 to June 1995, we took up the Seventh House segment. The Out Breath Signature or Seventh House cusp is "An Indian woman rowing a canoe and gathering wild rice." Each relationship, each dyad subsequently became the stark focus of this cycle. Theanna was instrumenting a change in the way men and women connect during our transformative times. In order to do so, she had to confront both Ellias and Alita with outer- and inner-world disruptive factors. As these were precipitating, we had somehow to sustain our momentum and send a love current through us into the glut of old ways manifesting everywhere. We could force nothing on the outer domain, but it was our destiny to work hard inwardly to bring an impulse into the world, one that was regenerative, all-encompassing, and true to the needs and destiny spark in each and every being.

When interpersonal dramas became inescapable and repetitive, Theanna concentrated her beam of world-renewal upon Ellias. She was orchestrating a mighty Merlin awakening through him, one which would snowball for years and years to come. The combined, as-one presence of Theanna and Alita allowed the ancient, timeless Merlin essence to be incarnated again into the world, to infuse everything we were doing with a magical puissance bonded to the Living Earth.

Where previously the cosmic domain was where we all found Theanna and stayed at one with her, the nature of her presence began to shift in the Seventh House cycle. She came to us more from within the Earth. Our intent was now to keep on penetrating the space she manifested and bringing it more into true incarnation. The challenges we encountered here were so daunting that only a very partial coming down through the veils was yet possible.

In early May of 1995, Ellias appeared in Santa Barbara for a conference called "A Matter of Life or Death." Theanna chose to attend with him. On the outside, the conference involved the usual ritual of people talking together about important matters, entering into a shared experience. On the inside, this was an ideal moment for Theanna to impart more than she could in a mere telling of her story. At the conference she worked closely with a few souls, assisting them through changes yet to manifest on the outer level.

The actual subject of how the dead can bring new forces to the living was not yet part of the collective awareness, so we completed the Seventh House experience with a big question mark. What was it going to take to reveal to the living even the smallest measure of what we were experiencing and transiting through?

At that time, we were on the way to writing and publishing *The Book of Theanna*. In that text we were seeking to express in a much broader sphere what we now were being renewed by everyday. We were going to tell the world that the dead have not gone anywhere, or certainly have not been obliterated; they are powerfully here. The obstacles to expressing something so outrageous apparently would prove to be great.

Alita, Theanna, and I were now in love, flourishing in hard times, expressing and embodying a cosmic revelation within a fairly ordinary, business-as-usual world. There were lots of humorous touches. Theanna was shifting her focus to where the living were stuck. Now that she was no longer in one of their bodies, she kept sensing over and again how impervious to real spirit presence human beings in the Earth tend to be; yet she was more than willing to blast through these barriers, in whichever way could do it and still leave everybody free and intact.

The Sixth House

From June to December 1995, we went under the horizon, fathoming ever deeper and further into the Earth, through the Sixth House. We were encountering the Old Earth, juxtaposed to the New. The cusp degree here—20° Capricorn—"Many different perfumes carried by a breeze"—exposed us to all sides at once relentlessly. Negotiating with an editor around what would be included in *The Book of Theanna,* we met a thought form that was collectively astute, gauging the marketplace of the 1990s for transmillennial books such as ours. As Alita, Theanna, and I imprinted this thought form, keying on what is politically correct, what is in tune with the trends of the times, we found ourselves wandering into a very paradoxical terrain. Other voices—voices of friends and allies—were backing up this pragmatic influence. What would we do in response to the reasonable demands of others that we fit within some kind of container, and submit to the rules of the Outer Earth?

We had to face in ourselves the shadow of self-righteousness. Even Theanna was compelled to confront a remaining residue of a certain kind of fanaticism. We wanted our own just-after-death cosmic impulse, as reflected in the letters, to be purely what came through to the living. Cutting out a number of letters and sections and wordings was almost too much for us. We were tempted to view the situation in a false, even selfish way. Finally we had to agree, we had to let the marketplace (the collective) decide. We were coming from a place that had no right to assert special privilege. This was the test we were undergoing. Would we fall for the thing for which spiritual movements always fall? Would we set ourselves above? Or would we acknowledge that what we bring is hard to take through people and must not be tightly held to on its own terms?

The planet Venus rides the Sixth House of the Theanna Prenatal Epoch. There are no planets in her Seventh, Eighth, or Ninth Houses. For the first time, we were called to face the much more substantial intervening presence of Theanna in this world through her Prenatal Venus. It gained momentum in the Fall of 1995 and bears the degree 23° Capricorn—"An old priest using oil to anoint a carved stone lingam." With this cycle, something else started to happen, far beyond what had previously seemed possible.

Theanna had been gathering her internal resources, while making sure not to impose, to leave everybody free. Then she struck. Alita and Ellias consummated the Alaska journey with a briefer Mt. Shasta excursion. In mineral baths, up on the Mountain itself, and again, while visiting with a savant lady, we sought merely a conventional renewing power. Theanna had other ideas.

She got inside of both Alita and Ellias, tapping an Ellias individual cycle to get him to perceive the many ways he was not yet being there or bringing what was needed into the shared stream. Simultaneously, Alita was plunged into her first full awareness of menopause, with erratic hot flashes. The body became the primary focus. We had to come to Earth, not the mountaintops of old.

The Venus propulsion was pentrating for months. We could not get away with much of anything. We were in the direct presence of a goddess who meant business. She sought now to take up her actual authoritative position. Here to mediate mysteries through her, Theanna was hierophant.

The Fifth House

From December 1995 to June 1996, we absorbed the far greater densities of the Fifth House. Theanna's cusp here is 20° Sagittarius—"The changing of water into wine." This indeed became our path from that point forward.

Each Easter and each Christmas, Theanna would write the Christ Letters. During that Christmas of 1995, we became far more deeply dedicated to the path of the Living Christ, a dimension that saturated every morsel of our experience during this cycle. In particular, this meant that we entered upon a sacred sensibility—a whole different Christianity than we could ever have dreamed up, or remembered, or tried to hold to.

The Christ Within Us took charge of our lives. We were meeting Theanna now in Christ. This meant that we had to be as her completely. Somehow, before this cycle, both Ellias and Alita had assumed that Theanna would carry the bulk of the spirit load and we would work with what she brought us. Now we knew our path was to be just like Theanna. She went before to prepare the way—and we were summoned to follow her way out of our own true light-essence.

Very early in this cycle, we came upon the South Node or Dragon's Blood of Theanna in 19° Capricorn—"A half-eaten piece of bread." *The Book of Theanna* went out into the world, and we were launched upon an entirely different destiny expression. Everything said, suddenly and without any possibility of missing it, that we needed to become the true embodiment of that book in every way.

No hiding behind Theanna's cloaks, we had to grow up fast. Ellias was called to speak, to lead groups, to work with material that had been published in new ways. To do all this in Christ was to walk in the world without masks, shields, identities, frameworks, any way to defend the self against what comes to meet it.

In the first round of these challenges, Theanna was right there with us. In fact she could be right there with each one in the room. If someone read her book truly, she could meet with that soul in the spirit light. Theanna began to belong to the whole of the Earth—and in the process, all of us had to go with her and become like unto her.

The Spring of 1996 brought Theanna's Prenatal Mercury into very immediate, tangible expression. The degree is 5° Capricorn—"Tall, dark cypress trees in a cemetery." Time had come for the death mysteries to be invoked, to be directly fathomed, in a new way. At first nobody could quite conceive what we were driving at. Even we ourselves needed to be sure what we were doing and why.

The Easter letters that year made it starkly clear. We had to bring death in the New Christ Mysteries to a world that could not yet hear and feel what we were saying. That is, we had not only to teach the world what death really is; we had to bring it into life by being it. Additionally, the task was to keep evolving within this matrix, neither worrying about who "gets it" nor withdrawing to our own safe precincts. And that rhythm became the Mercury dynamic, the metric which we move with always.

We never can be sure what is useful and helpful and what is too much for people. But our guidance shows us to align with the Christ Within, be true to Theanna's example, and let the world become as it needs to, without loading every situation with overwhelming expectation.

The Fourth House

From June to December 1996, we landed through the Fourth House into both the Old and the New Earth. The Old Earth landing was surpassingly strange. Just at the right moment the New Earth unveiled that we had come to be in it, and that we could alight safely into a world to which we actually belonged.

The Root Signature, or Fourth House cusp is 17° Scorpio—"The mountain abode of a hermit." We were truly landing in Merlin's cave. During the Summer of 1996, we wanted to believe that we could find that geological place or at least go wherever life led us. Yet we still had to come up against something unmapped and learn the crucial lesson of them all.

Theanna's Prenatal Sun, in the same degree as her death Sun, comes to meet us sharply here. It is 14° Sagittarius—"A terrarium filled with carnivorous plants." Theanna's impulse in this Earth is a very warrior-like one—to come right down into the thick of the collective chaos of the twentieth century, and to grok what it was that drove everybody crazy, to find the antidote to that poison within, and to bring it to this world in a form it cannot refuse.

The Book of Theanna had begun to reach many people, some of whom came into touch with us. Yet as we would work with them, the same dilemma we had been up against in Alita's world was there at another angle. People weren't really present because they did not know what this meant. They could not remember or envision what we were pointing to. Many liked the *idea*. But if they just applied our example in their lives, the old stuff stopped cold what we were insisting upon. After so many similar episodes, we had to realize that our message was too radical, revolutionary, and beyond how people saw themselves.

There followed, closely on the heels of this Solar blast of ice-cold reality, Prenatal Mars in the degree of 7° Sagittarius—"Rats with ruby eyes." The mass consciousness of modern America, the world we were all so accustomed to, felt as though it were spitting us out. What we bore as Theanna-seed, as Christ Mystery, as future wavelength was colliding with gross collective experience. Perhaps nothing so outwardly dramatic as that portends—but we were seething with the feeling that we needed to be in our own world somehow.

We traveled that autumn to England—a journey beyond any dreams. The ethers of the British Isles welcomed us into a deep-body feeling of suddenly and always belonging to this planet. It hit us like a tidal wave. In Avalon, we conceived a spirit child, a being who, after her birth in July 1997, became the pivotal focus of our evolving stream. Meanwhile, in ourselves, we were giving birth to many future possibilities. Ancient karmic events in this part of the world had sent us flying far from each other.

When we returned from ancient and timeless England, we now were deep inside the hermit's abode, Merlin's Cave. The depths were claiming us profoundly. Theanna was Vivyen was Theanna, entering her ancient self and bringing it back alive. We were entirely shattered, yet rewoven at the same time.

In the Fall of 1996, we could tell that a whole different way of being was seeking to come alive through us. This was a daunting challenge. We had to go back and start over. But how could we do this? We had worlds, selves, lives. What would allow us to pioneer such an entirely free space? Where would we find the place within ourselves that could be that bloody real?

The Third House

From December 1996 to June 1997, we were hurled through the Third House. The cusp of this house is 18° Libra—"A woman carefully counting the beans in a jar." Alpha Omega (or Chiron) is also in that degree, at the start of the Third House.

The pivotal event in this cycle happened mostly in the recondite depths. In Hawaii in February, Ellias became violently ill and spent eight days inside a volcano of a karmic intensity never previously glimpsed. Inside that psychic chrysalis spewed out was a gyrating proliferation of images, impressions, and agonies. Eventually this turned out to be a sudden, drastic immersion in the dark side of Theanna's past. There had always existed inside of her a suicidal impulse. At its most extreme in ancient Hawaii, this had been ritualistically enacted. Now it was everywhere, at the core of every subsequent lifetime, always with the sensation of drowning and of losing everything in a tragic heartache sense, fused at the same time with the fate of the Hawaiian peoples and extermination of Pacific Island culture.

When Ellias returned from these Hawaiian nightmares to the mainland, he was a different man. He never again could enter upon his soul link with Alita in a substantial sense. He had become so totally at one with even the darkest shadow of Theanna that he had to become in a sense her mate, before he could be with anybody else.

The Third House had been Sara's great catastrophic collective magnet. This time around, in the renewed Theanna mode, something altogether new was working through the events at hand. Alpha Omega can crash every party, yet bring forth, in the wake of that party needing to be over, a much more beautiful energy and awareness wave.

And so it was with us. We could not keep everything as it was. The depths had exploded everything we had tried to create.

Something new took on form of such a radical depth presence in Ellias that Theanna could at last venture further through in him. She had to use her own death shadows to carve out a space, at a very primal level, where Ellias was ready to let her through. We were entering a fermentive cycle—and Theanna needed to be in it, way further than anybody could admit.

When this was entirely forged in that Spring of 1997, Ellias emerged bearing Theanna within himself, extraordinarily at one with his core nature. Together they found themselves in a world where the kind of chaotic turbulence enacted in Hawaii was showing up everywhere. Those who kept count could say that the world was at the brink of something surpassingly strange. We knew we had to be as one to guide some small portion of this planet through the seething waters. Alpha Omega had fused the furthest polarities. The living and the dead had coalesced. We sensed and felt and knew that we were here together to last and that we belonged.

The Second House

From June to December 1997, we walked into the pivotal house of the Theanna Prenatal Epoch—and so we entered upon the most decisive events of all. The cusp influence is 18° Virgo— "Eyeglasses which cause one to see rainbows." Our eyes were wide open, our responsiveness acute. First we needed to move through the veil of one of the asteroids to get to the center of this maze of events. Ceres, the pivotal planetoid, is in 17° Libra—"A very bored woman who is listening but falling asleep." For a brief moment there in June of 1997, we experienced a vibrational fade-out world where anything we said or did got played back to us as though we were enveloped in cotton several layers thick. As we pierced the illusion, we got ready for a cosmic encounter.

This is marked in the chart by Neptune in 7° Libra—"A group of old ladies gossiping excitedly." Savitri, the spirit child of Alita and

Ellias, was being born into the world, opening a time tunnel and beginning a different era by her presence here. All of us were beside ourselves with the energy of it. An earthquake heralded the assignation. The etheric radiant presence of Savitri filled the room, filled the world. It was July 14, 1997. We were flooded by a redemptive spirit light. For weeks, all we really could do was to navigate through the subtle ethers with a feeling tone of something at last here *in the world,* something that could make a huge difference, something that had been totally obvious and totally absent.

Vesta follows closely in this chart in 4° Libra—"A woman bites into a lemon and makes a face." The world that Savitri entered, the world that Theanna was seeking to penetrate, was swept backward in time rapidly by "personalititis," the disease of the late twentieth century.

Many souls were bonded in Savitri's birth; yet all of these souls lost one another very fast. Each one spun to their own edge of what it all meant. Vesta revealed that, in order to be able to go forward genuinely, we were still needing to go backward.

Pallas in 28° Virgo—"Autumn leaves pressed in a book"—took the Vesta lessons a leap further. As summer turned to autumn, each one on Earth lived in their own scrapbook, their own memory pictures. People did not yet know how to keep company with a Savitri, to embody through a Theanna. It was conscience time. All of us needed to check ourselves out, clean up whatever was old, and get ready for a different world.

The final planet of the sequence, and by far the most powerful, is Jupiter in 26° Virgo—"An old man counting gold coins." During the Fall of 1997, Theanna and Ellias came to a place together where we could unite our forces in an emergency mobilization to met crises on every hand. This was an extraordinary cusp. We had to internalize everything that Savitri was bringing to the world. We had to turn it right away into useable currency, relevant resource. Everybody around us was splitting open, and we unwound from the inside, providing something substantive and resilient, a taproot that could be a source place from this point forth.

We felt lucid, centered, humbled. Everything that had been shaking free we had to make our own. We could not deny, suppress, objectify, project, nor could we take it on in a personal sense. What we needed to do was truly be there and trucking.

It was a very shaky time, strange and devoid of places to rest. Yet oddly enough, Theanna and Ellias were now an amalgam being, coming through with precision and elan. We knew what was needed, and we knew we would be there.

The First House

From December 1997 to June 1998 we arrived within the sphere of the First House. The cusp degree, which is both In Breath Signature and Prenatal Moon, is 18° Leo—"A rose bush. Many buds, but no flowers."

During this cycle, Theanna came to live with Ellias—not Sara but Theanna. She showed up one evening in a star class and moved in. She was there at bedtime, all throughout the night, on into the morning. Her sober, deep presence changed everything so fundamentally that it had to be a true miracle.

At first, all the embodied demonstration of this was in and through Ellias. He needed to get it together and to be supported at a level of intensity and commitment by Theanna. His own inward destiny path needed to catch up with what four years of bonding with Theanna had worked all the way inside and through him.

Every single night, there would be energy exchanged, communications given, guidance implanted. In the midst of the night, Ellias could feel Theanna there beside him. None of it ever varied even slightly. And so there began to arise on the inside, on the In Breath, a remembrance, a realization, a way of being. "So this," he thought, "is how the dead return. No wonder everyone thinks no one sees them. No one is looking where they are."

The initial form of it was that Ellias could unite with his own true body, tapping it as a magical portal into all the places he needed to go. At the center of this shamanic impulse, Ellias was being asked by Theanna to come to himself as never before and be like unto her so substantially that he could bear her entire essence with him wherever he went.

As is optimal for the timing grace of the First House, this cycle allows very little outward emphasis and dictates very intensive inward focus. This became so deeply true that the Spring of 1998 was the first season during which Ellias could contemplatively unite with Theanna at all levels and know where this was taking him and keep going there. Finally the mental explanation and skeptical figuring were over.

We were seeking to forge a fused self on the In Breath; we didn't require any external props or reflections. Nonetheless, a woman came along who could see and feel and know the entire essence of what we were doing, and she could reflect this accurately and objectively. When we allowed ourselves to rest within her reflection, we knew that our fusion of the greater Cosmos and the Living Earth, even if it was subtle and inward and deep, was becoming a manifest reality.

Destiny was stamping our combined stirrings as legitimate and enduring. We neither claimed certainty nor doubted. Yet the sober, lucid reality was that we could come through (May 1998) and be what we truly are together.

We had previously been in collective situations that were increasingly saturated with doubts, fears, questions. What was real? Where would it all go? Savitri had doused and permeated us with a fresh wave of evolutionary forces, designed to test and temper and get rid of whatever was no longer real. All of us were in the hopper, even Theanna in a sense.

We actually preferred it this way, for we did not wish to get caught in our own subjective vision. We welcomed the testing action. We were a little hard to swallow (ask our cohorts). There was a sense in which we were a future self, not prepared in the collective mind. Our motivating spark was beyond the world of the now. The darkness so many felt could not beguile us into it. We were on fire with a new world. And now we were starting to be entirely ourselves.

The Twelfth House

From June to December 1998, we were deep inside the Twelfth House. The Twelfth House Cusp is 20° Cancer —"Many brightly colored tropical fish." We were way to the inside of the collective. Most of this was such an extraordinary spectacle that we could just barely keep up with it. The key moment came early, with Pluto in 11° Leo—"A boy removing a thorn from his foot." This is the only planet maintaining the exact degree in the Sara birth chart and the Theanna prenatal chart.

Moving into Pluto in the Twelfth House was an absolutely astounding experience. We were privately publishing *The Christ Letters,* putting out feelers for a new communion of which to be part. In the direct interior experience of June and July of 1998 we were faced with what the world had become at the end of the twentieth century. It was time for us to be right there in it and to extract the poison from Ellias's flesh. Surgery was in order.

Human relationships were heavily polarized, even more densely than we had ever dreamed. We met in our immediate connections a growing sense that we were on our own and could not depend upon a community to house our radical new shared self. Theanna was now hugely insistent upon coming all the way through the Ellias physical vehicle. Nothing was to keep her out—no further postponements, no excuses.

Theanna had begun to spend a great deal of inner time with Savitri. Right away Theanna intensified her passion for working the magic, moving into and through the body. An urgency took hold of everything. The world around wasn't moving in a true progressive direction. We knew it would and that we had to keep the faith in the meantime.

When you're in the Twelfth House, and you've fused together within a novel collective imagination, a theophany, the only way you can steer clear and attune is to trust and believe in your own experience, even if it goes wildly against what others are reflecting. In the Fall of 1998, we found ourselves squarely in this predicament. We took a car journey to the Northwest. Although we were beautifully and poignantly met by friends and people with whom we could work, somehow everybody seemed to us enveloped by a time bubble. Something vital was missing.

Returning from that journey, we could not go on in the California way. Something absolutely different again needed to happen fast. In November of 1998, all worlds were ending. What would be the fresh impulse?

Ellevera, involved with many of these events for years leading up to this point, came directly before us, bearing a radically future-fertile way of feeling and being. If we could help her to cast off the semblance-persona of these times, she was there with us, willing to discover what Ellias and Theanna were in a total, shared sense.

One of those peculiar Twelfth House moments followed. We were faced in Ellevera with a direct answer to our prayers. Yet how could this be? Just as was true with the same timing in 1993, when everything was lost, grace was ripe to restore the essence and bring something entirely unexpected with it.

Ellevera had this capacity to meet with Theanna and Ellias, without ever splitting us or making us seem to be these two independent entities. She knew who we really were. The wildest part was that she could be the link, the completion of a whole new triad. In a very rapid, stunning way, the future opened wide.

The Eleventh House

From December 1998 to June 1999, we became a shared future organism in the Eleventh House. The cusp says it all—20° Gemini—"A bull stung by a scorpion." Death, the scorpion's sting, was at long last able to pierce the skin of the living, the thick Taurean hide. By the combined desire, need, longing, and willingness of Ellias and Ellevera, what Theanna had been trying to infiltrate into us all became so inescapable that it showed up everywhere.

Very early in this cycle, the Ascending Moon node or Dragon's Breath burst into resonant expression. This degree is 19° Cancer—"An opossum comes out into the moonlight." Matching the power of the Dragon's Blood *Book of Theanna* publication three years previously, Theanna now strode forth into the world of the living as the three of us together. She was entirely different from what she had previously seemed. This new form was obviously her true, pure manifestation, with no parts littered on top of it. The Theanna we came to know from this time onwards was an utterly inward being. She presented herself to us as raw elemental stuff from the depths of the Earth. Her whole auric emanation was of she-who-is-at-one-with-the-planet-and-its-living-waters. Here the personified homunculus-goddess was intact, whole, absolutely naked and unadorned. It blew us all away to meet Theanna as she truly is. It would have blown us away to meet anyone in this primal state, free of any clouding embodiment.

Saturn came roaring along with its testing action, yet also with its multi-worlds power. The degree is 10° Cancer —"A violent hailstorm." We appeared on a radio program with an interviewer who was a depth psychic. Right on the spot she tuned into Theanna and gave a direct reflection of what she met. The being she revealed was so loving, so accessible, so real, so affectionate, and also so demonstrative that we just could not keep Theanna away from us ever again.

Soon thereafter, we were in the car on the way to giving a public talk. Theanna suddenly began to speak of a Core Earth Curriculum. She gave us the first two guidelines—more to follow. In that public talk (and all subsequent events), working the Core Earth Curriculum became a cornerstone of our entire process. We were absolutely on fire with future seeds, with the living presence of Theanna in our midst; yet those not so psychic tuned us out successfully.

A death of a very close kin to Ellevera gave us an edge on the situation, a fresh death momentum. We would need this badly, as here came Juno in 6° Cancer—"A medusa's head with writhing snakes for hair." The Spring of 1999 still had for us lots of horror shows to digest and entangle with. The Earth was coming out of its science-fiction cloak, yes, but *into* its science-fiction cloak again, both of which were neither. From all possible and hypothetical and falsely New-Ageized and spiritualized futures, one vivid, simple, fully tempered reality was shimmering into being—as lucid on the inner plane as a landscape transmitted electronically back to Earth of the outer plane of Mars or a moon of Uranus. What was real proved to be just as surreal as the real could not be, thus was only momentarily surreal, each moment, before it zinged into utter, more than eidetic realness.

Most crucially, we were now pellmell upon our star book *Inside Star Vision*. The class that met to work with the material in here was by far our most responsive and in-tune group ever. Each couple of weeks, the book and the people and everything linked with this momentum pulled us forward.

Amazing people, fascinating energies and awarenesses all the same.... The mind, the head, the thought forms of the America-enwrapped world-obsession were killer. People everywhere were driving themselves crazy with manipulated media images of Y2K and every other disaster. On a personal scale, there was some kind of bug going around that made everybody miss the living future, the one we were directly inside of. Instead the apocalyptic, faux-Mayan techno-hate cinema was playing at every marquee. The pages of the media listed no other feature, no alternative event.

Yet this stuff was as hollow and rootless as a tumbleweed. A real molten rainbow firelikeness bloomed just beyond in the actual desert-tundra.

Savitri began to write us Future Keys letters, for a whole different vision to be shared, the true affirmative one. And we were here together, stronger and clearer all the time. We brushed off the collective mind dreads and fears, and we did unite with a bright future.

The Tenth House

From June to December 1999, we were moving through the Tenth House. As we wrote this text in July, very powerful planetary forces were at work in this transcription and its ripples.

The Crown Signature, or Tenth House Cusp, is 17° Taurus—"A pomegranate broken open." In transmitting these free-form reflections, we are directly breaking into underworld, a hidden-away vista, never to be fully revealed out-in-the-open aspects of Theanna's destiny fable. We are bringing her back from the dead, far more alive than the pseudo-living of the late twentieth century.

But in this moment, we are meeting two decisive planets, the final two in the sequence. First, in writing the Sara karmic tale, we were inside of the Earth Under, in 14° Gemini—"A sorcerer materializes an amethyst cross." And there we found that magic, miracle, redemption, the impossible come true, death leading to rebirth. These things could not be reduced to reasonable terms. The living story had to reveal itself in its own impossible stretchings.

Now, in writing this and the final chapter, we come upon the leading planet in the pattern, one we call a Catalyst Chart—two-thirds full, one third empty. This planet is Uranus in 12° Gemini—"Many huge urns filled with wheat." We'll conclude this account with a reflection of what Uranian influence is really like.

All the cycles we are sharing in this chapter (as I write) were freshly revealed to us in recent days. This entire tale is something that tells itself by coming from way deep inside all of us. As we allow the total cosmic picture, in Uranian terms, to manifest in our midst, a truly staggering portrait spreads itself over the whole for the whole to see at last.

We are now embarked upon an infinite future. Sara was intensively Uranian. Theanna is just as Uranian. Yet in 12° Gemini, we find such rich treasures, such abundant stores that you could never exhaust them. This is what has happened in the soul and spirit of Theanna.

Sara used to run out of energy quite easily. Theanna is a storehouse of collectively regenerative forces. We share these experiences in order to give her away (what else could we do with such a cornucopia?). For we have learned in recent years that we can never possess anybody or anything. Most especially, Theanna does not belong to Ellias and Ellevera. We are just here to give her a place to land and to come from. Her destiny is boundlessly plentiful. All our destinies are.

We will go through the same houses one more time in the next six years. But this time around, all of it will be universal, wide open, free. From the moment she returned into the world of the living, Theanna has been bursting all shackles. With support from Savitri, she is now ready to break us all free.

Can we believe what is said here? Are these things possible? Is this a kind of alternative something that is a little different from the New Age, the Esoteric, the places people look? Or is it just more New Age flotsam, and we some more blind, itinerant wanderers across the cosmos' overwhelming broad and vast face. Are we yet onto something here that is infinitely alive?

Can it be that death is a conveyance into everlasting life? Can it be that this springboard is now being offered freely to the living as well? What would change if this were true? How about everything! Everything doesn't say it. How about...how about if everything became only what it actually is?

All we can say inside the Tenth House is that we stand behind our words; we are here in this world, and we mean to be a bridge to a stunning future.

SAVITRI
PRENATAL EPOCH
SEPTEMBER 30, 1996

ELLIAS MERLIN
PRENATAL EPOCH
AUGUST 15, 1946

CHAPTER 3

Vivyen Future Cycles
— in Synchronization with
Savitri, Ellias Merlin, and Ellevera Shane —

The Year 1999

Duing the course of the first six years after the Triple Death, Theanna gradually shed her pure cosmic essence in order to align more closely with the soul of the emergent New Earth. To mark this, she took on ever more fully her ancient timeless Earth name of Vivyen. We will now track with Vivyen's further cycles in a new vein toward the future.

Besides the pure Prenatal Epoch house cycles moving backwards (tracked in the previous chapter), we are going to be keyed now on special transits to prenatal planets. Vivyen will be joined by three close companions on her journey, so we will take prenatal cycles for all four.

Each Vivyen companion embodies a planet beyond Saturn. Vivyen will be tracked through Pluto. Ellias Merlin will be tracked through Neptune. Savitri will be tracked through Uranus. And Ellevera Shane will be tracked through Alpha Omega—Chiron.

We look toward key conjunctions and sometimes oppositions from the above planets in their transits to each one's Prenatal Epoch. We intertwine common synchronized cycles in fully prophetic fashion.

The focus throughout here is to see the future, not to predict it. We have learned ways to extend our senses through imaginative journeying wherein we are shown directly by spirit what is meant to unfold in a given sector of time. Our foremost interest is to invoke the collective pattern broadly and then to reveal likely breakthroughs, all centered around Vivyen's pivotal impulse to forge a new world. We will let most extraordinary factors speak for themselves. Mind-stretching is in order here, to let the future in.

During the latter part of 1999, our only pivotal star cycle is Neptune opposite Ellias Merlin's Prenatal Saturn. This Saturn is in the Eleventh House in 2° Leo. The Chandra symbol is "A horn of brass to be used as a hearing aid." Here is what we see coming in this vein.

Because this year collectively is a number one Cat or Rabbit year, we interpret this as collectively the doorway into the future, yet blocked in a certain sense by each one's rational mind and the limitations we place upon human potential in the twentieth century. The future is at hand, but few let themselves go there in 1999.

In November, at the culmination of almost two years inside this major transit, we see Ellias Merlin going through the portal of what the entire twenty-first century is to be and becoming awake to it in a multi-sensory quickening that matches ancient trance and grail states and brings them forward anew. We sense this as quite a vast tuning in through a core crown opening to faculties previously dormant or only half-explored. It is as if the great stone cathedrals at Glastonbury, Teotihuacan, and Monte Alban and the serpent mounds of Kentucky and Ohio were to come alive both as organs in flesh and chakras enveloping organs.

Ellias Merlin is our Neptune embodier because he, with his Prenatal Venus conjunct Neptune in 7° Libra in the First House, is entirely at home in bridging, accessing, and integrating multiple worlds. He was given a thirty-year Neptune initiation from 1969 to 1999, in order to be entirely sensitized to all the worlds converging toward the future. It is in this end of twentieth century Saturn moment that he can bear great collective fruits from that initiation.

Vivyen has been fostering a very different Ellias from anybody he had ever been able to conceive previously. Now he is future-focused in each moment. It is Vivyen's touch to make sure her star mate is entirely grounded in the Neptunian mysteries as she reveals these to him in rhythmic stages lovingly.

The Year 2000

Collectively, the new millenium opens onto a year keyed to the number two, which is also the keynote of a long cycle to come. We see this as the transmutation of the Moon through the power of the Divine Sophia. We are shifting our collective lunar trance, which was keyed to the mists of remembrance and forgetfulness, into a wholly different Moon sensibility aligned with Sophia. The whole of existence is in a Divine Mother embrace from a wise and willing place. This first year wheels right into the shift.

The year 2000 is a Dragon year. Such years are high points when we realign with our greater nature and aspire to come forward in a very different style—so this is collectively a radical new beginning at a higher octave.

Ellevera Shane will be experiencing Alpha Omega or Chiron moving across her Prenatal Mars in 13° Sagittarius. In the same cycle, Ellias Merlin will be inside of Neptune opposite his Prenatal Mercury in 6° Leo. Let us see how these cycles become interwoven qualitatively as opposed to linearly.

Ellevera Shane is one of these souls who came in at the right moment in the twentieth century to hit her stride just as the twenty-first century rolls around. In her instance, this was very wakefully chosen before birth, for she was entirely here for the twenty-first century and could experience every moment of the twentieth as a sentencing to go way back and endure the Old Earth. For Ellevera, this transit represents her first real activation in this lifetime. Ever since the Triple Death, Vivyen has been preparing her inwardly to be ready for major threshold work in times when life and death are meant to come together in radical ways.

Ellevera is Alpha Omega because whenever she contacts any given angle of future access, of inner opening, right away her innate predisposition is to find a resonant point—wherever that might be—and link her entry node there. She can never settle within a personal or individual claiming of what is here. Her body knows that she is just a point along the way and is here to provide a communion contact between and among realms that need to find one another again.

Her Prenatal Alpha Omega is 7° Aries—"A double-headed eagle; the heads face in opposite directions." To go here is to be aware of the other point there, awaiting fertilization: no isolate separatisms; only linkages and connections, making futures possible.

In this 2000 cycle, Ellevera's Prenatal Mars in the degree of "An embalmer at work on a mummy" will pierce through to a harmonic remembrance of how we worked with life and death at the peak of Ancient Egypt. From that place, she will forge, in her own desire and active embodied expression, a link with Vivyen's Awakening Dead.

The Ellias Merlin cycle opposite his Prenatal Mercury in the degree of "A hamster running in a treadmill" shall be able to track, record, report, and make a navigational practice out of the breakthroughs Ellevera comes to in the year 2000. In fact, his path will be to be so energetically attuned to the subtlest nuance of what Ellevera is coming to with Vivyen that he can then make all of this universally accessible as precisely what the Awakening Dead ask of the Living. It will be time in the dawn of the new era for the brightest promise we come to at death. That is to be here for the Living, at hand in embodied substance.

The Year 2001

Collectively, it will be the year 2001 that gives us a feeling for what the Twenty-first Century is all about. This number three year opens a future door much more emphatically than the threshold year of 2000. We are invited to expand our range of life expression to a much greater spectrum of possibilities. In particular, while we activate whole new ways to be, we are asked to transform and transmute what is no longer in sync with progressive evolution.

This is a Snake year. Everything is on the inside, involved with the hidden, the subtle, the previously denied. We are given the chance to rediscover and reintegrate many forgotten places. The ancient, the future, the timeless present all become one.

Vivyen's key prenatal cycle occurs in the year 2001. Pluto goes over her Prenatal Sun, which is also her Death Sun, in 14° Sagittarius—"A terrarium filled with carnivorous plants." But first let us see why in-depth Vivyen embodies Pluto.

The innermost power of Pluto is to cleanse and purge all outward-ly-conditioned patterns by providing such a strong inner-worlds pres-ence of core spirit that external syndromes disintegrate. This is Vivyen Pluto, under a barrage of new evolutionary force. It is, as we have seen in previous chapters, in the same degree natally as prenatally—11° Leo—"A boy removing a thorn from his foot." In the Twelfth House, a collective thorn is being removed. Our thorn is that we can't walk onward alone; we need convincing and near spirit accompaniment. In the initial phases, the Dead, the twice-born, have to show the way.

As Pluto goes over Vivyen's Prenatal Sun in 2001, she seeks to bring the fruits of the Triple Death into universal currency, right into the thick of the most densely packed and constricted situations and con-texts. This is an inward impulse; it is not about external dramas or crises of the usual kind. What the Dead awaken in the world of the Living is so strong that the course of evolution is altered founda-tionally.

Ellevera Shane synchronously has Alpha Omega on her Prenatal Pallas in 25° Sagittarius—"A boat with no one in it slowly drifting out to sea." It is the destiny of Ellevera to be there on the spot when Vivyen is ready to embody the death mysteries for the Living. Ellevera will crack herself open to such an extent that there will be nobody here to limit or relativize the full dimensional impact of what Vivyen forges and substantiates.

In the aftermath of previous cycles this shall be the moment for the liberating vibrancy of awakened death forces to reveal to the Living how to follow the same track. It shall be the moment of complete readiness and willingness to move with beings of light where they show us we need to go. Ellevera will be selected to funnel this death wave through into the Living, just as it comes through.

By 2001, the idea of death and the Dead and all the other dull deadly phrases in their domain will be supplanted by a real feeling for what is involved when we move to the inside of life. Twice-born, awakening ones view the Living not as the Living but as once born or fledglings. In a sense, we who live stay as children. It is the path of those who die to unite with wisdom and truth at every turn. They become our elders, Universal Tribal Elders. Every Aboriginal people, unblinded by civilizational lights, has recognized this in the pure dark of the soul's night.

The Year 2002

Collectively, 2002 is a number four year. This is the most grossly misinterpreted of numbers. It bears the sign of a quickening of the collective pulse, an impulse to take up the wave of future awareness and begin to forge a new world with it. Major steps to reverse the entire collective situation begin to manifest in this cycle. It is a hub of turning points.

2002 is a Horse year. This means all directions open, all possibilities revealing themselves, everything calling us onward as we can actuate to meet it. The most dynamic, direct energies come into play. The brighter future transubstantiates what we still carry from the past.

Savitri experiences Uranus opposite her Prenatal Venus this year. Why is Savitri Uranus and who is she really?

As we have briefly introduced previously, Savitri is the daughter of Ellias Merlin and Alita, and she has lived in the ethers of the Earth since July, 1997. She is the eldest sister of the Children of the Future, all of whom (except her) are physical-blood beings come to regenerate the human species and buoy us all beyond our previous limits.

Savitri is Uranus because she is living vision enacting itself in every way it possibly can. She is the boundless scope of cosmic awareness brought to Earth. Savitri's Prenatal Uranus in 1° Aquarius reveals such a powerful threshold impulse into the future that she is the pivotal figure in ordaining and instituting what can be fulfilled.

For Vivyen, Savitri represents the one who does for birth what Vivyen does for death. Through Savitri, the portal of birth is being liberated from collective blockages into a truly wide-open door for the most evolved to enter.

Savitri's Prenatal Venus is 26° Leo in the Fourth House —"A fire burns at the bottom of an old well." During 2002, this ultra-pivotal year for all of us, Savitri is going to be finding homes for the most radical future spirits and also beginning to introduce the close members of her inner family to selected members of the Children of the Future. They will walk together with and be in tune with us during the coming cache of years.

Ellevera's Alpha Omega will move into her Third House, passing through the cusp this year—5° Capricorn—"Tall cypress trees growing in a cemetery." This is Vivyen's Prenatal Mercury degree. More than anybody, Ellevera is here to bridge the span between the twice-born Awakening Dead as elders to the tribe and the Children of the Future, the ones who will carry the torch of evolution brightly forward. From this time onward, both companies will feed into each other through Ellevera, and we will discover how they can mutually complement and embrace and surround the living from both sides.

We have seen ourselves coming to meet the Children of the Future in 2002. What we quarry there is a depth of aliveness, a formidable backbone of bringing boundless spirit into every inch of Earth existence. In these visionary encounters, we already feel that these are our kin, our living born-through-us destiny, guiding our lives now, bringing us toward them through Savitri pervasively.

Savitri will speak for herself in her own letters and books. But it might be relevant here to indicate that her depth has spread into the first thirty years of the Twenty-first Century, helping us all to get there with her. Her broader scale impulse begins to distribute its seeds all the way through in 2002—the harbinger of the gladdest tidings. She is making where we need to go just about inevitable.

The Year 2003

Collectively, 2003 is a number five year where we enter a new world and discover a different way to live. The constraints, the programmings, the denials filling recent centuries now lose their grip altogether. We are plunged into a zone of innovation, fresh creation. This decidedly depends upon our co-creative willingness to participate, to be all the way here in the Earth. This is landing time in Planet Earth, setting sail for the future, the real future.

This is a Sheep or Goat year. The entire mass culture, the whole collective scenario is what we must take up, take on, take through us, spit back out. It is time to free up the ways we always assumed life had to be. Uprooting false and distorted patterns is crucial.

When Sara died, what she renewed with her life mate and now star mate William was a cosmic connection that could bridge across life, death, and all apparent separations. She became Theanna Vivyen and came into full authority of being able to work in the Earth from elevated planes through the body of her mate, who became Ellias Merlin.

In 2003, Pluto goes into Vivyen's Fifth House, piercing through the cusp—"The changing of water into wine." This is the moment when the incarnational capacity of Vivyen in Ellias Merlin becomes entirely embodied and lived. The Christ miracle is enacted afresh. Vivyen can now blaze through without obstacles barring the way.

In the same timing, Ellias Merlin moves through his fulcral cycle of the coming years. This is perfectly intertwined with Vivyen. Neptune goes opposite his Prenatal Pluto in the same degree as his Natal Pluto—12° Leo—"The mouth of the Amazon River," which is also Sara's natal Venus degree. This concomitance seals the total connection between Vivyen and Ellias Merlin.

How will this core partnership evolve in its greater working? We have already heard a summons to do our ultimate kind of shared work, together with Ellevera. This could well involve, for example, being brought to Avalon, to Glastonbury, in England, to complete some ancient Merlin work, to take it forward from here.

Our foremost impulse is to collaborate with the soul of this planet to throw off all false outer husks and regenerate herself at inner-most root levels. If the right spot in the right timing is given the appropriate activation magically or alchemically, the Earth can be stimulated to remember her own essential way of being and to reinstate this upon a fresh evolutionary spiral. Once we are at full strength, the work of the future will bid us into the vaster cycle of service on a global scale. This is the convocation everyone has been awaiting, although few have been aware of it.

Vivyen's Fifth House activation in the Christ Light suggests that current timeless Earth work must be in fullest accord with the New Christ Mysteries, or with what is seeking to emerge in the future spiritual dawning of this planet. The sacred dimension shifts the Arthurian stream just enough to pop all kinds of worlds loose from their false polarizations and old deputies and disputes.

Ellias Merlin's Pluto activation in the Eleventh House opens a portal into the vaster future of the human species and of all living beings who share this planet. We shall be dedicating ourselves to sustaining the long range prospects for a wholeness of being to flourish in this planet for any and all who seek such a way of life. In 2003, all facets shall combine forces to make a much more vibrant and palpable life pulse.

The Year 2004

Collectively, 2004 is a number six year. This asks us to gather together in groups and new ways of serving. A borning world requires a boldly innovative approach to what will serve the future, what is truly relevant and timely. This is the year for the most visionary and far-reaching alternatives to surface and give of their substance to the common need.

This is also a Monkey year: The moment is called. The stage is set. It is the time for displaying what has been long gestating prior to this cycle of emergence. No further hidden clauses and escape hatches, just about anything and everything we need to know will be right here.

In Vivyen's inner family, this is Savitri's year. Our only key star cycle is Uranus moving into Savitri's Eleventh House and passing through the cusp—5° Pisces—"Thousands of gold nuggets glistening at the bottom of a clear stream." For Savitri, this is a literal representation of what is directly at hand. Let us give the narrative over to her for what will be unfolding in 2004.

A time tunnel opened at Savitri's birth. It closes in July of 2004. That seven year time passageway was a protective sphere to make future initiatives possible within an opaque collective cycle. That dark transit ends in this year (2004), leading to the following scheduled event on the cosmic calendar.

At a large site still to be determined, a thousand souls will gather, most of whom have not seen each other in the physical domain this time around. The oldest among them will be six or seven years old. These are the Children of the Future, in their first annual convocation, to be together and do the service they can best perform.

Each member of the tribe we call The Children of the Future is primed before coming into Earth with one very special gift or treasure to hold within as a marker—a tone, a song, a sacred sound. This is Heavenly future music that needs to be heard in the Earthly world.

When these future children gather in a large arena, they will record for the larger world the songs, the tones that all remember as one. They will be a children's chorus, sounding the Earth toward its optimal future state. This song will then be released across the dense and polyglot habitats of civilization, to be heard and felt and known. It will be how the Children of the Future let the others know that they are here and that they bring the deep sound that restores the feeling of who we are here and where we are going. In the collective media we have seen cartoonlike portendings of this global harmonic and transdimension encounter with our future selves.

Savitri's Eleventh House opening heralds a virginal quickening impulse. We have arrived at the prearranged time. A few of the more mature will accompany the many. They are young in body, ancient timeless in spirit, and future visionary in their souls.

The other end of the vestibule, 2004, is the prelude toward the final phases of the Piscean Age. It is new genesis when we will all begin to realize our true nature. The restoring of all essential vital things is at hand.

Savitri expressed the vaster future horizon. The exordium to a boundless future opens wide. Wherever the Children of the Future are rooted and nurtured, they will bring a light and a tone into the world that changes our very structures. "The Sun-eyed children of a marvelous dawn" have arrived.

The Year 2005

Collectively, 2005 is a number seven year. This is the point in the cycle for internal catching up. Each one of us is thrust on our own to process the wild times we are in and to revel in a new place from our own spirit core. It is a reaping cycle. What has been gathering in the years from 1999 is now entirely manifest and can be gathered and used as a springboard ahead.

This is also a Cock or Rooster year. We are brought before the vaster worlds and asked to speak our mind, offer our contribution, reveal what we have come to and what we intend. The spirit forces are going to be very prevalent this year. Their agenda is entirely about becoming at one with total purpose and design of the mundus, this world.

In Vivyen's intimate circle or inner family, 2005 is a year for Ellevera Shane. Alpha Omega goes over her Ceres, which is a pivotal influence in the Prenatal Epoch, squaring both Moon on the In Breath and Saturn on the Out Breath. Its degree is 1° Aquarius—the same as Savitri's Uranus—"A two headed calf." In basic star terms, the future seed impulses of Savitri in the previous years now become a total reality for Ellevera.

In our vision of prophecy, let us say a very close friend of ours is dying. Ellevera and Ellias Merlin, together with Vivyen on the inside, attend the days of the dying process. We get completely involved in the current of what this remarkable soul is moving into. As we assist her in crossing over to the inside of life, we are there with her so completely that this cannot be just another death journey.

When our friend goes out the Crown and chooses a high spirit death, Ellevera Shane instantaneously accompanies her across. In full consciousness, after previous trainings and extensive preparations, Ellevera goes with our friend and directly shares all that she comes to in those initial hours after passing inward.

There then arises a shared impulse between this friend and Ellevera to walk back into the land of the Living together. They move back and forth a few times. Both beings are as one living or dead, once or twice born. Soon it is clear that Ellevera can embody with this woman the next stage, the one for which the Triple Death makes way.

The unification of life and death is not a single epiphany. It requires many passages back and forth, like a bee in flight among the many flowers of the field, carrying a invisible thread, alchemizing an interior nectar. This time around, life and death are co-equal partners, balanced, symmetrical, in tune with the whole journey as one. Ellevera becomes a wide-open conduit for the threshold impulse of the Awakening Dead. They stream through her at a whole new level. And then it happens.

The barrier cracks. The worlds embrace completely. There was an ancient agreement for the inner ones and the outer ones to co-create the future of this planet. It is at last fulfilled. There is no further question or distance. And so Vivyen can sow in the soul of our friend who has passed inward a radical impulse, an impulse which could not quite activate back in 1993.

Because Ellevera is so fluent and open and well-schooled and because our friend is truly ready for this as well, the new times are fulfilled by a fresh, awake spirit impulse piercing through into outer Earth and revealing what is meant to happen here and how we all can partake in a revelation that is both pure vision and dense Earth embodiment, hardy and viable. A New Heaven and a New Earth are palpably coming into being.

The Year 2006

Collectively, 2006 is a number eight year. The complexities of this number are almost incomprehensible. In one direction, this is a threshold of extremes. It keys on playing out all factors previously missed or neglected. In another plane, eight shows a mastering of pivotal lessons and a stage of coming forward into capacity to be and do whatever is asked in a very rich, multi-dimensional expression. On yet another axis, the eight makes all the darkest and heaviest and most volatile collective components something profoundly present and shared, something we are all in the midst of and cannot moderate or minimize. In a further dimension, eight is ultimately the year of mutational breakthrough, where the open door to the future is accessed and brought into common currency.

This is a Dog year. Such times are reserved for taking a step forward and staying resolutely with the previously unknown realm . It is a practical time, a chance for the New Earth to take root in particular ways forging constructive directions for everybody who helps form the web of the New Creation. This is that time for implementation, application, making it work. And this clears the decks, opens the space, makes whatever comes next something we all can work toward, with shared intent and brotherhood/sisterhood capacities mobilized to the max.

In Vivyen's immediate circle, we have no major planetary activations in 2006. We are far too busy implementing the initiative of the previous year. The only thing we can do now is to inhabit both worlds, where those in bodies and those in subtler bodies live, and bring these worlds together so tangibly that nobody anywhere can miss it.

The year 2006 is a really deep entry point into extended cycles to come. We see the years up till 2012 or so as the dawning of the Aquarian Age. And then in 2011 or 2012 or 2013, or all of these as one, the real Age of Awakening begins.

We are looking toward that time as ushering in a nodal window, a thread of eighteen years or so of the seeding into an entirely different evolutionary dynamic. And whether it is the Children of the Future or the Deep Earth work, whether it is forging life and death into one or taking these star studies to their ultimate fruition, we will be there with all of us, as the Earth becomes a bright star once again and is welcomed into the Galactic Federation.

It is self-evident that we do not focus upon struggle and strife, disaster and cataclysm. For we are convinced that the twentieth-century dark read-out on the future is its own contained message to itself, saying we can't stay in this mode of consciousness much longer! So we bid a fond good-bye to the doom frequencies of modern times and welcome in the vision beyond ancient prophecies, the future itself. The twentieth century talking to itself about the twenty-first century can be many things, but it cannot be the twenty-first century (though it can pave the way to it by undermining faith in the long reign of quantity and stastistical mass and its commodization of existence itself).

Vivyen and her growing intimate circle are formed around a simple basis: All of us in here together share the awareness that the Earth is moving into its grace cycle and solicits help from all the lost and missing parts. It needs partnerships to flood the parched lands of modern intellect with an entirely different sensibility. And we are willing to move wherever spirit asks, for we are not prisoners of ideologies or points of view.

Vivyen herself, Sara Theanna, is the story. She has started something. Many are in on this now. We offer it to everybody else, with no strings attached.